Tea Cups
and
Cowboys

~~~~~~~~~

One Mom's Journey with
Laughter and Tears

Kendra D. Graber

ISBN-10: 0615581293

ISBN-13: 978-0615581293

This book is dedicated to . . . .

My Lord: He has proven Himself faithful and all praise must go to Him.

Lowell: For letting me try an idea that was planted in my heart years ago. Thanks for supporting me through this, hon. I just know the rest of our lives will be as exciting as the last twelve have been. I love you.

Derek, 10: For being my obedient, responsible son. Thanks for helping me with the little ones so much and for doing it with a cheerful attitude. You are such a blessing!

Terrel, 8: For being my sweet, vivacious boy. You have provided quite a bit of the material for this book and have warmed our hearts many times over with your humor and antics.

Megan, 7:   For being my darling daughter.   Your calm personality and girlish manners are much needed in this house. You are precious beyond words!

Logan, 5: For being a balm to your daddy and me during the past four years. God, in all His wisdom, knew what He was doing when He gave you to us. You have provided so many moments of joy!

Wyatt, 2: You were our prayed-for baby and have brought us much happiness!

I'd like to thank Denise Wurm who, out of the sweetness of her heart, edited this book at no cost.   It was very much appreciated! And a big thanks to my friends and family who encouraged me to write this book, as well as those of you who read it and gave me your honest opinions.   Without you, I wouldn't have had the courage to pursue such a project as this.

Table of Contents

Foreword

Foreword

This book came about because of my friends and family. We moved 2,000 miles away from both sides of our family in 2006. After we moved, I began sending back e-mail messages to those who wanted to hear about our life in northern Idaho. The e-mail list kept growing and some even suggested that I put them in a book. So here it is. I have taken some of the stories contained in those messages and added a few more besides.

The bulk of this book was compiled in the winter of 2009. Soon afterwards it was shelved because life got really busy with our fifth baby on the way. The little darling is now two years old, so I decided to dig this book out again.

Several things are different now than when I wrote it, but I wanted to keep the original draft the way it was. For example, we now send our two oldest boys to our church school instead of homeschooling them. I like to homeschool kindergarten and sometimes first grade, and then send them to our private church school. Also, we've added another child to the family and he isn't mentioned in here by name. Despite the minor discrepancies, I hope you enjoy taking a peek into our lives.

I do want to thank those of you who encouraged me to write this book, because I probably would not have done it otherwise. This project has taken quite a bit of time, but I pray that it will be well worth the effort.

Chapter 1

"I Do" Before Diapers

Once upon a time . . . As a young girl I loved reading stories that began with this line. A beautiful princess falls in love with a dashing young prince and they live happily ever after.

Happily ever after meant that they never quarreled over the right way to put the toilet paper roll on the holder. The princess never gave her prince the cold shoulder for the time he gave her a birthday gift a week late. She never grumped about how that dashing young man left piles of dirty clothes on the floor next to the laundry hamper. And he never forgot to open her door to let her out of the car . . . excuse me, I should say "carriage." He never got irritated with his princess when she nagged at him to get the dryer fixed or the light bulb changed or the sink drain unclogged. *Happily ever after* just doesn't happen. Or does it?

I met my "prince", Lowell, when I was 19 years old. My family had moved from California the previous spring, so we were new in the area. My mother, sister, and I were attending a Christmas program at Lowell's church when I noticed him. He was standing in the choir singing with such gusto and animation that he even caught my mom's eye, although she didn't tell me about it until much later, and the thought crossed her mind that Lowell would make a fine man for me.

A month or so later, we were together with some youth our age. I stood there watching him, although he had no idea I was doing so. I began to hear a whisper in my heart. God whispered that this was the man. And I listened. I listened very well that time.

Now perhaps I'd better describe him to you a bit so you can understand exactly what follows. My man is a "grab the bull by the horns" kind of guy. He will take an idea and jump into it feet first, sometimes even before he's checked to see how far he's jumping. He is a man with an on-and-off switch. It's either all-out or nothing for him. He works big, plays big, and sleeps big. Nothing is done in baby steps.

We are like the story of the hare and the turtle. I am the turtle. He is the hare. I will plod along doing my own thing in a slower, methodical way while he is miles ahead of me, although perhaps down a rabbit trail. Contrary to the hare-and-turtle fable, we both arrive at the finish line about the same time, even though he has run more miles in the same race, had more exciting experiences, and used up a greater number of calories. And I daresay, he also had more fun than I did!

He is like a kite flying high in the blue sky, seeing the world from high above with all its grandeur and possibilities. And I'm the one holding the string down on the ground. He yells down to me what great visions he sees while I stand there looking at the string in my hand.

He hears every side of a story before making a judgment. I tend to pick the side that makes the best story and stick with that one. He sees the whole picture, while I'm hunched over with my magnifying glass. He runs. I walk.

He has gone snowboarding, rock climbing, and motorcycle riding. I am content to putter around in my garden, plant flowers, or read a book. So, you can see that we are two very different people. But we fit together like a "hand in a glove!"

Now that you know his personality, it will come as no surprise to know that it was only a couple months later when he asked my father if he could date me. And it was just barely more than five months after that when he asked to marry me. I said "yes," and about nine months later, we said "I do!" And I haven't stopped meaning it since.

I wanted this chapter to be the first one since it is the chapter upon which the diapers are founded. "I do" needs to come before the diapers. Do things in God's order, and you will be forever blessed.

Marriage is one of those things in which you will work

the hardest, cry the most, and laugh the longest. You will give until it hurts.

And then you'll give some more.

I have now been married more than a decade. Twelve short years in which I have hurt more and loved more than I ever have in my life. It has not been a piece of cake. Nobody's marriage is.

But it can be a piece of heaven if God is Lord of both of your lives. That is the key ingredient to a happy, fulfilling marriage. He is what is missing in the homes filled with abuse and divorce today. Without Him, it might be a happy marriage, but there will always be something missing. Jesus.

Marriages "made in Heaven" still take a lot of earthly work to keep them there.

"Wherefore they are no more twain, but one flesh. What therefore God hath joined together, let not man put asunder."

(Matthew 19:6)

Sanity Tip: *When your prince leaves dirty dishes on the couch or wet towels all over the bathroom floor, go take a look at your wedding picture. Remember again why you married him. Now go give him a big kiss!*

Chapter 2

Honey, I'm Pregnant!

"Honey, I'm pregnant!" So far, I've gotten to say these words quite a few times. And, to his credit, with none of those words have I ever had to pick Lowell up off the floor, although a couple times, he seemed to turn an interesting shade of gray.

It always strikes me as rather unique to the male gender that they seem to think this baby is coming overnight, because usually the next word is "when?" Perhaps it is because they are the more logical of the two genders. When they want something, they go out and get it right then. We women like to dream about what we want, then change the color, shape, or size of it, and then scratch it altogether and dream of something else. God has humorously given us women nine months to dream about the little bun in the oven—what color, shape, and size it will be—only this time, we can't change a thing about it. We just get to dream.

Soon after seeing those two pink lines, all those wonderful, glowing feelings transform into other feelings. Other feelings that leave absolutely no doubt that I'm pregnant.

Morning sickness. Just the word can send shudders through a woman. You picture a woman hanging over a toilet bowl with dried puke on her face and a green tinge to her skin. Now I have never gotten that bad. I just feel nauseated all day long and sometimes all night. I'd rather hole up in my bed for three months than go out and cook that bacon or change that messy diaper or take out the stinking trash.

Then there is the moment you look in the mirror and realize that your tummy is not nearly as flat as it used to be. Yet it doesn't look like you're pregnant either. Instead, you just look sort of thick. That's when Lowell gets tired of me saying, "Honey, I look fat!" No, you're not fat, you're just pregnant, you hormone-laden woman. He has never said that to me, but it is true, nonetheless. Hormones seem to warp our brains while we're pregnant.

I've even heard a rumor that pregnancy kills a few brain cells. Of course, it is just too much fun having something else to blame for our blonde moments. Who wants to take personal credit for the time you burned the hamburgers, didn't put the right amount of sugar in the cookies, or mislaid the bank statement? No, it's much more convenient to blame it on pregnancy.

One of the greatest, yet frustrating wonders of pregnancy is the little built-in heater the baby has become. It's great if you are nine months pregnant in December. But it is frustrating to be nine months pregnant in the heat of the summer. The rise in body heat is one of the first clues to Lowell that another munchkin is on the way. In a non-pregnant state, I have cold hands and feet. So when I start having warm hands and feet, he begins to look a little worried.

I don't know about you ladies, but there are some nights when I'm pregnant that I just cannot sleep, either from the baby moving around in all regions of my anatomy or from the craving for cookies and milk at 2 a.m. I've had both of those, by the way. One of my babies was such a wiggler that, in the last month, I had to sit in the rocking chair and rock him to sleep before he was ever born! And I've also had a pregnancy where I'd wake up in the middle of the night and couldn't go back to sleep until I'd had a cookie dunked in milk.

Once you reach your ninth month, you realize why a pregnant woman waddles and why bending is nearing the impossible. And then there's the awful problem of getting out of bed. Lowell likes to tease me about being a beached whale for those times when it's much easier to have him heave me out of bed than to try it on my own.

But all of these troublesome woes of pregnancy dim when you feel your baby move the first time. There is no other feeling in the world quite like this one. Your months of feeling sick to your stomach twenty-four hours a day are rewarded by that first little flutter. You finally realize that there truly is a baby in there, and it's making its presence known! Soon that flutter becomes a poke, which turns into a kick, and then about the eighth month, it begins to feel as if the baby is using your bruised ribs as a punching bag.

Then there's the labor. "Honey, I think it's time!" We ladies finally get to see what color, shape, and size our little package has become. And the men breathe a sigh of relief that, finally, they might get their wives back from this "disease" that has transformed them into something other than what they married. All the cravings, complaints, and moods of pregnancy will surely be gone, and life will be just like it was before.

Wrong. Real life is just beginning. And none of us first-timers are ever ready for it.

So we speed away to the hospital where I am hooked up to all kinds of wires and gadgets until I feel more like a science experiment than a woman about to give birth to her baby. After all the initial work is done on me, we are commanded to wait. And so we wait. And wait. And wait.

Soon Lowell gets bored with all of the waiting and decides it's time to eat. Out he goes to bring back a Papa John's pizza, which I have to smell from across the room while I'm sitting there watching those mountain peaks they call contractions.

Finally, things begin to happen, and our first little boy is here! And wouldn't you know it that, just as Lowell is trying to get his first diaper on him, he messes himself right there on the changing table. Perhaps that should have been a sign to us as parents that raising kids isn't for sissies.

So we take our home and begin life with 12 a.m. feedings, 2 a.m. feedings, 4 a.m. feedings, and so on. And just when he's turned one year old, two pink lines show up again. "Honey, I'm pregnant!"

Again, we go through all the pregnancy joys and woes until it's time to head to the hospital once more. Well, since last time took so long, we figured that this time we'd do some of the waiting at home. Except we almost waited too long.

It was raining cats and dogs when we left for the hospital. In fact, it was the storm of the decade, according to the newspapers. The roads were flooded and trees were knocked down, but we made it to the hospital ER entrance. Lowell dropped me off at the entrance doors so he could go park the truck. I had to wonder how many people were holding their breath as I waddled through the ER waiting room, expecting my water to break at any minute.

Since the rain had flooded the hospital basement, the elevators weren't working, and so they showed us the stairs. Now for you ladies who've been in labor with contractions every two minutes, you'll know how hard it was to climb three flights of stairs. But there's a silver lining with every cloud, and about an hour later, our second son was born! Daddy didn't even have time to go out and get his pizza. Oh well, maybe next time.

About 10 months later, I had to tell him yet again, "Honey, I'm pregnant!" Now I do believe that this time shocked him, but he had recovered quite well by the time he had to drive me to the hospital once more. This time we took no chances of a baby being born in the truck, in the ER entry, in the elevator, or in the stairwell. The doctor induced me, and three hours later, we welcomed our first little girl!

Now here is where life took yet another interesting and challenging turn. We moved 2,000 miles away from Lowell's boyhood community in Indiana, plus both sets of grandparents, and many uncles and aunts. All of our moving plans were going along great, until one week before our departure date when I had to give a piece of most shocking news: "Honey, I'm pregnant!" I don't believe that was exactly part of his moving schedule, but he had recovered by the time we arrived at our new home. They say when it rains, it pours. And we were sure getting wet.

This time we were clear across the continent and had to choose a new caregiver. We decided to try a home birth since the last two had come seemingly fast. Actually, I was trying to keep Lowell as far away from a pizza joint as possible. So eight months later, we had our third little boy right in our own snug house in the mountains of Idaho. There were no stairs to climb and no flooded roads to drive on, although Lowell continued his tradition of eating while I was having contractions. Only this time it was Pepsi and corn chips.

Next time I'll hand him a breath mint.

"Good things come in small packages." (Aesop)

"And God blessed them, and God said unto them, Be fruitful, and multiply, and replenish the earth, and subdue it...."

(Genesis 1:28a)

Sanity Tip: Enjoy your pregnancy! Slow down and take time to savor the miracle God is working within you. It will only happen a few times in your life, so relish every moment.

Chapter 3

Clean Houses Don't Exist

Friday morning—cleaning day. I've had my coffee and am raring to go. The children know to stay out of Mom's way on Friday mornings, especially if I've had my espresso. Out comes the vacuum, the broom, the mop, the dusting rag, the window cleaner, and all those nasty-smelling bathroom cleaners that about make you puke, especially if you are two months pregnant at the time.

Usually the children are sent to a remote part of the house when it comes time for mopping. But invariably one of them will venture back to that alluring sight of a shiny floor only to have reality hit them bottom first when they wipe out on my clean linoleum. Little size-four footprints can be seen all over the floor until the spot where the little tyke realized it wasn't as fun as it looked.

Now I wouldn't call myself a clean freak, meaning, I don't need to clean every corner of the house every week or get every speck of dust off the mantel. But I do like my toilet clean, which is hard to accomplish when you have three little boys in the house. I can have that toilet just as sparkling clean as the picture on the toilet bowl cleaner bottle, come back after two boys have used it, and wonder if I should just install an outhouse in the backyard.

You moms probably know what I mean. Sometimes it seems as if they are aiming behind the toilet instead. Middle-of-the-night potty breaks are the worst, I do believe, especially when our Terrel was about five years old. He was one of those who sleepwalked to the bathroom and yanked down his pajamas with his eyes half-closed, and the rest was left up to chance as to where it happened to land.

One of my favorite things to do on cleaning day is light my best-smelling candle to help freshen up the house, especially after my pie dribbled over in the oven the previous night and filled the house with a horrible smell. Then I walk through my sparkling house and enjoy that wonderful, clean smell before something happens to break my trance. Something such as a little boy running inside from the sandbox with a rubber boot full of sand or a little girl who drops a jar of yogurt on my shiny linoleum or the littlest tyke decides it would be great entertainment to step on that cracker on the carpet.

I have yet to time how long I can keep my house clean on a Friday morning once the broom is put away, the mop is out to dry, and the crumbs have all been vacuumed up. I do believe I have reached the five-minute mark, but I can't say as I've gone past that.

I've decided there are two ways you can deal with something like this. You can fret and stew and make the children feel like they can't even live in their house or you can turn a blind eye and go smell that candle once more. That's hard to do, but it will save your sanity in the long run. There is absolutely no way a house is going to stay the way it looks in a

Good Housekeeping magazine when four children are running around, eight hands leaving fingerprints on the windows, and eight little feet bringing in mud from the creek.

We moms just have to realize that this, too, shall pass. And the time will come when there will be no more happy voices coming from the sandbox, no more chubby faces pressed against the glass, no more laughter coming from the bathtub while water gets sloshed on the floor, and no more little hands that "help" make cookies. Let's enjoy these memories that we are making, even if they are memories of a yellow puddle behind the toilet!

Don't sweat the small stuff.

"To every thing there is a season, and a time to every purpose under the heaven." (Ecclesiastes 3:1)

Sanity Tip: For a quick, middle-of-the week swipe over the bathroom, use a wet towel left over from a kiddo's bath time to wipe dust, dirt, and puddles off the counter, toilet, and floors.

Chapter 4

There Were Four in the Cart

and the Little One Said

I'm not a window shopper. I do not find it relaxing and exciting to walk around in a store looking at things I will not buy. What sense is there in that? But send me into Wal-Mart with a long list of items we need and the checkbook, and I'm in shopper's heaven.

I'm a listy kind of person. Now being a listy person does not make you a righteous person. No, in fact it's quite the opposite. We who make lists do so because we need them. Without them we would be totally lost. We have a sort of brain deficiency when it comes to remembering if we needed milk, or was that light bulbs? No, maybe it was refried beans. Come to think of it, it might have been toilet paper. See what I mean?

Send me into a grocery store with no list, and I'll inevitably come out with way more than I needed, will have spent double the time from trying to remember what was on that list at home, and I'll get home and discover that I already had half of what I purchased. Send me in when I'm hungry and with no list, and that spells disaster—at least for the checkbook and my diet. Every box of macaroni and cheese looks scrumptious; even those dill pickle chips, which I 'usually can't stand, look rather good; and while checking out a box of Lucky Charms, I'm dreaming of the ice cream on sale in the freezer aisle.

So that's why I need a list. In fact, I can pull out several grocery lists from my coat pocket a week or so later, although they usually are a bit crumpled or discolored, especially if they've been sitting too close to a used Kleenex.

Now that I've got my list all made out; the diaper bag is full of diapers and pull-ups, bottles and sippy cups; and, of course, my wallet, I'm all set to go. When we get to the supermarket, we have two choices for grocery carts. One style, which holds one child but more groceries, or the other style, which holds four children but fewer groceries. It all depends on how long Mama's list is, if she's had her coffee, what speed she's in today, and, ultimately, if she wants the groceries or the children hanging out of the cart. Most times, we choose the one where more kids can get in since they make more noise than groceries do when they fall out of the cart. When the next child comes along, I may need to invest in some sort of trailer to pull along behind.

Everybody's in their proper seat with arms and legs inside, and so we begin our shopping. Mama's trusty list comes out of her pocket, gets stuck between her teeth as she picks up the potatoes, gets stuffed back into the pocket so she can get the little tyke's bottle, and then comes out again once we reach the meat section. A couple times, I've come close to panicking when it seemed that I had lost my list. But usually a tiny pair of hands had grabbed it, or I'd stuck it in the wrong pocket, or had absentmindedly put it on top of the eggs where it slid down to the bottom of the cart.

Now if you're a wise mama with four children in the cart, you know there are certain aisles that you either do not go down at all, or you go down them so fast that the grocery store police might ticket you for speeding. Things pass by in such a blur when traveling at an increased rate of speed that the children don't realize they passed the candy until they are on the bread aisle.

But then you still need to get past the sugared cereal. If a couple months have passed since we bought some sugared cereal such as Lucky Charms, we'll splurge and stop there to decide which fake breakfast food we would like to rot our guts this time. And here's where the quarreling begins. One child wants Fruit Loops while another wants Cap'n Crunch. Daddy likes Lucky Charms, but little tykes eat the marshmallows first and then grump their way through the "healthier" aspect of that particular cereal.

Once we've gotten half of the things marked off of my list, it's usually time for the potty trainee of the group to yell, "Mom, I gotta go!"

How fast we get to the restroom depends on how advanced they are in the potty training stage and the tone of voice in which they yell it. If it's just a whine, we probably have two more aisles we can squeeze in before heading there. But if it's an extremely panicked tone, we need to be there in about thirty seconds flat. Usually we leave the cart, and everybody takes a trip to the bathroom, but once in a while, the one yelling needs to go NOW, and so Derek, our oldest, gets to watch the baby while we run to the restroom.

I came out one time to find the baby standing up in his seat on the front of the cart with a sweet, old lady standing there, probably wondering where this poor child's mama was. I was only gone a moment but long enough for the baby to show his independence.

Another time, I parked a little too close to the wine bottles, and the littlest guy decided he would like some. I caught it just in time to set it back on the shelf. I was not in the mood for champagne, thank you very much. Besides, it wasn't on my list.

Finally, we have all the items that we need. I didn't say all the items on the list. There' have been a few times when the stress level from taking four children grocery shopping has reached dangerous heights, and I've scratched off the few things we thought we needed just so we could get out the door a bit faster.

At the checkout, the children who can reach the check-out counter like to get out of their seats and "help" unload the cart. And those who can't see over the counter find it delightful to finger the candy that is at their eye level. After we make it through the checkout, we can finally get out to our van, load it up with groceries and kids, and go home.

I've often wondered if the supermarket manager has a sinking feeling when he sees our tribe headed through his doors. I probably would if I were him. Who *would* welcome the sight of a blond mama with four wiggling kids who wears out a path to the bathroom and a list that keeps getting lost a? We live in a small town with a small-town community grocery store, and I must say that the people who work there are some of the best people here.

Sometimes there are days when we should just stay away from the public eye entirely. Hole ourselves up at home so that we don't unwittingly ruin someone else's day, sanity, or property. One such time happened a couple weeks ago.

We were all going stir-crazy within the confines of our house in the middle of winter, so we decided that I would take the children to town. We left Daddy at home in the peace and quiet and headed off to the bakery to get ourselves a donut and latte. The children love going there but can sometimes forget their manners.

The donuts had been demolished, and we were headed out to our Toyota. Derek had his milk in his hands and was gazing up at the ceiling, not watching his milk at all. As his head went up, his milk carton turned down, and his milk spilled all over the floor of the bakery. I quickly sent him outside as the owner came to mop it up.

I tried to curb my irritation as we all got in the vehicle and headed to our Bible study. After that was over, we needed to pick up groceries. This time, we chose the cart with more groceries and fewer children in it. It was the pickle aisle we terrorized that day.

Megan was wearing a coat with a big fur hood that stuck way out back of her. As she stood in front of the pickles, she turned around, and the hood on her coat knocked off not one, but two fat, round jars of pickles. I stood there frozen! I couldn't hide. I couldn't even try to run away without anyone seeing us. All I could do was stand there gazing at those pickles lying so helplessly all over the floor in a big puddle of sticky juice.

I finally got my wits about me just in time for the store clerk to come walking up. I apologized and moved my children out of the way so he could mop it up.

For those of you mamas who take your children with you when you go grocery shopping, you have my admiration. It is not for the faint of heart. Yet every time you go is another precious memory made!

Good memories are our second chance at happiness. (Queen

Elizabeth II)

"Wherefore do ye spend money for that which is not bread? and your labour for that which satisfieth not? hearken diligently unto me, and eat ye that which is good, and let your soul delight itself in fatness." (Isaiah 55:2)

Sanity Tip: *I have debated what to put here since I'm not sure if there is a tip for reclaiming your sanity while in Wal-Mart—especially if your toddler helped himself to a Snicker bar, your potty trainee' is yelling at the top of her voice, and you realize that you completely forgot the milk, which was the reason you came in the first place. On days like that, I have thoughts like this: "It's only as bad as you make it," or "I know I will laugh at this later—but you sure won't catch me laughing now!"*

If there is one thing I could offer you, it is exactly what I just said. It is *only as bad as you make it. Sometimes I find that, if I expect too much out of my children, my shopping experience goes downhill in a blinding speed. But if I go and have fun with my children and they detect that attitude, we all come out with smiles on our faces. Somebody once said, "More is caught than taught." Let's throw our children a happy shopping attitude and hope they catch it.*

Chapter 5

Critters

Spiders I can handle. Mice, snakes, worms, rats—anything rodent or reptile—I cannot. Even frogs are pushing the limit.

But I'm afraid my children don't feel the same way. They will play with frogs and worms, although they haven't started in on the snakes yet. Mice are nothing to them. In fact, before I had boys, I know of only a handful of times that I saw someone actually hold mice in their bare hands. If it were left up to me, I'd either get out my gloves or throw the mousetrap away with the mouse.

One summer, Lowell was getting mighty irritated at them little buggers. They had found a way into his truck and were giving him the nastiest surprises in there. He was none too pleased that someone or something else had found his stash of Snickers! So he would set mouse traps under his truck each morning and could sometimes catch up to two a day.

Now, mind you, he didn't bother telling me the first time he decided to put those traps under his truck. Well, he pulled away for work one morning, and about three hours later, I went outside to hang up wash. To my utter surprise, I nearly stepped on one of those traps—with a mouse still in it! After shivering and shuddering for a while, I sweet-talked my two boys into picking up those traps and dumping them, mouse and all, into the trash trailer.

There was no way I was going to show them how to empty the traps—that's a daddy's job. After Lowell came home, he showed the boys how to empty the traps, and they actually got a big kick out of it. I'm wondering if it doesn't boost their male ego since they are a bit braver than Mom when it comes to rodents. Ugh. Makes me shiver just thinking about it—it must be something in the male blood to enjoy such a thing as that! I think Lowell can't wait for the day that the boys discover how much fun it is to scare Mama with those mice.

The boys are also learning about the food chain around here. I heard them laughing behind the house one day, so I opened the window to see what was so funny. Derek said they were watching the cat eat something.

I wanted to know what it was. In my mind, I was picturing a piece of trash she'd found lying around. So Derek scooped it up and said, "This!" I nearly fainted as he stood there with a huge grin on his face, holding a chipmunk or mouse or squirrel or rat or something. And it was still wiggling! It was a little half-hearted wiggle, but I *know* I saw it move.

Gasping, I ordered him to put it back down and come wash his hands. He got the most perplexed look on his face, as though he could not for the life of him figure out why I did not find this as amusing as he did. But he obeyed, bless his heart! I'm just not sure about raising boys and all that it entails.

Then again, our curly, blonde daughter probably would have done the same thing. She and the dog probably share cookies. Gross. Come to think of it, she loves to play with the frogs, too. And I know she most definitely did not get that desire from her mama.

But of all the critters to move into my house in Idaho with me, there are two I dislike the most. Mice and snakes. It seems we have one or two or three (or who knows how many) slimy, slithering garter snakes that like to surprise the tar out of me. They like to hang around under our front porch and in my flowerbeds.

You have to make sure before you put your hand in there to pull that weed if the weed is actually worth it, because you just might come up with a snake instead! I have nearly stepped on one in the grass, nearly sat Logan down on one, and nearly picked one out of the flowerbed. Needless to say, each and every time, my blood pressure skyrocketed and a scream erupted.

Now I haven't mentioned rats much because I have only had one occasion in which they got a little too close for my comfort. I was very newly pregnant with our second son, Terrel. Lowell was off on a hunting trip in Colorado, and I was trying to be brave in our single-wide trailer in Indiana.

One night, I was lying in our bedroom at the end of the trailer when I heard a horrible scratching sound coming from the kitchen. I had heard that at other times in my life and knew it was a mouse or rodent of some kind, probably trying to climb up the inside of a wall.

The following night, I lay down in my bedroom again only to hear something thumping and bumping on the floor in my room. From the loud sound of it running, I could tell this was either a mouse of gargantuan proportions or it was a rat.

And this was a tiny room. There was room for only one of us. Either the rat or I had to leave. And since the rat wasn't going anywhere, I took off like lightning for the living room couch to shiver and shake until morning.

The next day, I was walking into my bedroom and accidentally bumped my bed. It seems the rat had taken up residence there, and at my intrusion, shot out from under the bed, across the floor, and escaped under the dresser. From the split second I saw him, I knew it was a rat. And I was out of there.

I went home to my mama's. Where else does a young woman go when her man is not home to protect her from the wild creatures living within the confines of her cardboard house? That rat had proved to be a little braver than I. But I wasn't done fighting yet.

Before I left the trailer, I set out a whole pack of mouse poison on top of the washing machine. When I returned home a couple days later, the entire pack was missing! And the rat was gone, just in time for my husband to return home from his elk hunting trip. And, boy, did I have a hunting story for him!

A day is lost if one has not laughed. (French)

"O Lord, how manifold are Thy works! In wisdom hast Thou made them all: the earth is full of Thy riches." (Psalm 104:24)

Sanity Tip: *Try to remember the great benefits of having worms in your garden the next time you find one in a handful of freshly-tilled soil. I know someone told me they are good for the soil ... if only I could convince myself of it.*

Chapter 6

Vacation Deluxe

Ever since God has blessed our family with little ones, I have realized that at the same time, He also changed the meaning of the word "vacation." Vacationing is supposed to be relaxing in the hot sun at the beach, skiing down a mountain in winter, sipping a tall glass of iced tea in the south, or just sitting back enjoying the scenery while traveling along I-80.

Vacationing is not supposed to be full of potty breaks every hour, half-eaten hamburgers under the car seat, trying to keep the baby quiet while everyone on the plane is watching you, and taking a head count after every stop to make sure nobody gets left behind.

Then, once you actually reach your destination, nobody sleeps when they are supposed to, and then they do sleep when they should not be. Little immune systems get worn down, and we all catch the flu that's going around, as if it were a little welcome gift to us.

We are going here and there all hours of the day until, finally, we realize that we actually got more sleep before we left on this here vacation. Of course, it is still fun seeing all the family, friends, and sights we went to see. But it sure is a lot more work than vacations were before toddlers.

So far, we have tried vacations by plane, train, car, and Daddy's truck. I can't really tell you which my favorite is because they all have something in their favor. Planes get you there in a day. On trains, the kids can walk around more. By truck, you have your own schedule.

Before we leave on one of our truck trips, Daddy cleans out his truck until it looks perfect. And it stays looking clean at least for the first 30 minutes. After that, the level of debris behind the front seats keeps rising.

Every time we hop out for a potty break or McDonald's grease burgers, Daddy cringes at the layers of paper, pens, wrappers, dried french fries, toys, books, games, cups, bottles, and a soiled diaper or two that have taken over his truck. There is an art to opening those doors because you never know what is going to fall out—bottle, diaper, toy, or kid. Probably whichever made it to the highest level of debris.

After driving all day, Daddy finally decides he's had enough of us all littering his truck and pulls into a motel. Motels, for us, are never very sleep-inducing, probably because the children have inherited a genetic disorder called Noisy Sleep Syndrome. Two of our children are chronic moaners in their sleep. One child cries when his covers are on crooked. And, of course, the baby wakes up all hours of the night to eat or is popping a new tooth.

Daddy himself is the most interesting when he sleeps. He can almost hold a conversation, if you know how to speak his sleep language. If he's not talking, he's been known to laugh in his sleep. As for me, I don't know what I do in my sleep because I'm sleeping and it's already so noisy in there that no one would probably hear me anyway.

The next morning, we get our groggy selves up, eat our breakfast of continental something or other, and climb back in that truck. Then is when the kids want to know how long it's going to be until we get there. Problem is, we usually have two more days ahead of us.

Finally, after eight stops at McDonald's, twenty potty breaks, two motels, and numerous diaper changes, we arrive at our destination, worn out, but we hope with a smile on our ketchup-streaked faces. The children love going to Grandma and Grandpa's house back in Indiana. There are lots of toys to play with and oodles of cousins. Once they've all been played out or Christmased out, it's time to get back in that truck and go home.

Our one trip by airplane was quite an experience. The fourth munchkin had just arrived six weeks earlier, and we were headed back to Indiana for Christmas. We were going to be gone for three weeks, which we have since decided is way too long with four children. But we packed up all our suitcases and drove to the airport three hours away.

The littlest guy was in my front-pack baby carrier so that I could have my hands free to hold onto little hands or help Daddy with luggage. We all got to security and learned that we were required to take off our shoes. Not just our own shoes, but five pairs of shoes. And then two minutes later, we had to put five pairs of shoes back on. The airport security system did not have families like us in mind when they designed that set-up. And wouldn't you know it that, while they were scanning my diaper bag, they found a little pocketknife in there.

Now I did not want to tell the nice security officer that, at any given time, I cannot recite to you all the items living within my diaper bag. I shudder to even put my hand deep into a pocket for fear of what I might find, although more often than not, it's in the class of dried food such as a half-eaten cookie or already-chewed gum. So they confiscated my pocketknife, and we went on our merry way.

Once on the plane, the children did considerably well sitting in their seats. We had given each of them a little backpack to fill with a couple toys, snacks, etc. for the plane ride. I don't believe we had even left the runway before items started coming out of those backpacks.

We had one layover in Minneapolis, Minnesota. It wasn't much of a layover—just long enough to rush four toddlers through that airport of gargantuan proportions, go potty once more, change a diaper, and board our next plane. It's extremely interesting to watch other people watching you when you have four toddlers in an airport. I was ahead of the bunch with the baby in my baby carrier when a sweet elderly man stopped Lowell. He was admiring our three oldest children.

Then I turned around, and he could see there was a fourth. His eyes got wide and he had to exclaim all over again.

When we were landing in Indianapolis, our six-week-old did not want to be quiet. And that can be highly embarrassing and frustrating when you are on an airplane with several hundred people. They all begin to look at you, wondering how you're going to shut that baby up. Besides that, the seat belt sign was on, so I could not get up and walk him around to calm him down. Needless to say, he yelled for quite a while. But people were really pretty good about it—at least nobody started throwing things at us.

~~~~~~

Our trip by train was an even bigger adventure than the one by airplane. We had to get on our train in the wee hours of the morning over in Montana, so that messed up the kiddos' sleep schedules right off. But other than that, we were enjoying the train quite a bit. Until we reached Chicago.

We were supposed to take a smaller train out of Chicago to Renssalear, Indiana, which would be about a two-and-a-half-hour ride, arriving there around 9:30 p.m. Well, when we got to Chicago, we got off the train, found a place to store all our luggage, and went to find some supper. After supper was ended, we went back to our luggage pile to wait our turn to go.

Finally, it was time to get on our smaller train. So on we climbed and found our seats. The two littlest ones fell asleep while waiting for the train to depart. After a while, the train moved a few feet and then stopped. We sat there another twenty minutes until someone announced that there had been a medical incident although nothing serious.

Twenty more minutes passed and someone announced that the engineer had severely injured himself trying to fix something on the train, and so they were looking for someone else to drive the train. Lowell offered, but they wouldn't let him. (We actually found out later that the engineer had completely severed two fingers and was already in the hospital as they were speaking to us.)

After sitting on that train for a whole hour, they told us to deboard because in all of Chicago, they could not find anybody to drive the train, so they were going to take us by bus to our respective locations. So off we went, back into the lounge area to wait for another hour and a half until our bus arrived.

As you can imagine, the children were getting really tired of waiting. One of them was monkeying around and fell face first off of his chair onto the floor below. What followed thereafter sounded like a siren going off! And, of course, all the other passengers were looking at him with sorry expressions.

While waiting, I decided it might be smart to put the two littlest in their pajamas and proceeded to dig through our mountain of suitcases and boxes. Finally, it dawned on me that one suitcase was missing, the suitcase with the two littlest ones' clothes, diapers, shoes, etc.

Frantically, I told Lowell, who, after looking, confirmed that it was indeed not there. We had been responsible for getting all of our own luggage on and off the train, and it seems that we had left one on. He went in search of an agent to help him. Coming back, he said that the item was on its way to New York but that they would ship it to us when they could get it.

When our bus arrived, we piled on it and squeezed into our tiny seats and took off. The poor bus driver was going so fast at one point, knowing we were all grumpy and wanting to get home, that a policeman actually pulled him over. All of the passengers were feeling rather empathetic for the poor fellow. After all, he told us that he had left a pot roast supper at home and had to tell his wife that he couldn't pick her up at work because he had to come drive a bus for us.

While he was out talking to the policeman, Lowell was holding the baby, who was trying to sleep and drink a bottle at the same time. All of a sudden, the little guy sat up and proceeded to vomit all over the aisle, barely missing the person across from him. Now everyone on the bus was feeling extremely sorry for us poor people with sleepy, grumpy, barfing kids.

Finally, we arrived at our destination sometime around 11:00 p.m. My folks picked us up, and we still had to drive home a couple hours yet. We actually did get that suitcase back, which was a miracle, considering that it did not have a name tag on it. And the ride back home on the train went much more smoothly.

So you can see that vacations are not what they used to be. But it helps me a lot to remember, while I'm in the midst of a trying circumstance, that once it's over, we will laugh about it. That's something that keeps me going through tough times. You must make a conscious decision while you are in the thick of it to look for the humor in the situation.

Humor is a decision, not a reaction.

"Be glad in the LORD, and rejoice, ye righteous: and shout for joy, all ye that are upright in heart." (Psalm 32:11)

Sanity Tip: *When taking a road trip with little ones, take along surprise bags. A surprise bag is a small paper bag filled with goodies such as candy, balloons, stickers, a small toy, a snack, tablets, or anything your child considers a special treat. Make several of these bags, and get one out for each child when they are more bored than they've ever been in their life. It gives them something to look forward to and gives you a few moments of relative peace.*

Chapter 7

Mt. St. Megan Erupts

If there is one thing I absolutely dread about wintertime, it is being sick. It seems as though every winter keeps getting a little worse. One winter we had the stomach flu multiple times. Another winter we got a nasty respiratory flu and then kept getting something every other week until spring came.

If only the children would keep their germs to themselves, we'd all be much healthier. But that just doesn't happen with four kiddos with snotty noses who share cups, Kleenexes, baths, and slobbery kisses. Germs are a part of who we are anymore. It seems they've taken up residence within our household and indulge themselves in our pocketbook by doctor visits and medicines.

One of our best stomach flu stories occurred right after we'd gotten home from a trip. We were at some friends' place for a delicious supper of poor man's steak, mashed potatoes, green beans, and dessert.

I was enjoying every bite of my meal while holding our daughter, Megan, who was two at the time. We were sharing my plate, when all of a sudden she started up-chucking and wouldn't stop! I had a towel handy in which I quickly tried to catch the vomit.

With the first wave, I received a generous helping of regurgitated mashed potatoes on the side of my face and in my hair. I must have overreacted to that because with the second wave, I nearly rammed that towel down her throat in an attempt to catch it.

That was when Lowell received a showering of twice-seen food down his pant legs! He was holding three-year-old Terrel at the time, who also received a supply of vomit all over his feet. Terrel just sat there wiggling his feet and saying, "Yuuuck!" Poor Lowell, I wondered for a while if he would get over that.

After that tidal wave, I thought Lowell was going to go down and not come back up. He had to put up with the smell all the way home—especially when the van heater started warming it all back up again, for the third or fourth time. It did not help him any that I could not stop laughing!

Lowell kept giving me his side of the awful story, which only made me laugh harder. It really was rather hilarious, except for the fact that I *desperately* needed to wash my hair.

Then wouldn't you believe it, about two months later, it happened again. Lowell was lying on the couch with Megan sitting up on his stomach. She had been throwing up that morning, but I thought she was fine since she had held down some fluids. Well ... those "fluids" reappeared in a rather volcanic manner! And underneath all of that gushing liquid sat poor Daddy. Megan sure had it in for him that year.

Once I could see over the river of vomit, I really had to feel sorry for him and yet I wanted to roll on the floor laughing, except that my stomach hurt, too. I think he now has a permanent paranoia about Megan and the flu. He squeaked and squawked all the way to the shower, but I couldn't blame him any. He'd had his share of Megan's regurgitated meals that winter.

The next winter, we had the "real" flu. Most of the time when we talk about the flu, we are referring to a stomach flu. We had never had the real respiratory influenza before. But that winter we did. In fact, I think it was nationwide.

One morning Derek, our oldest, woke up with a high fever and then lay around all day, eating nothing and drinking little. The second day was the same for him. About that evening, I began to feel a sore throat coming on. Around three in the morning, I woke up to some of the worst aching and chills I've had since I was a kid. I ached clear down in my ankles.

That day, two others woke up with fevers, aching, and chills. We lay around for three days, taking temperatures, blowing noses, and giving out Tylenol.

Thankfully, Lowell did not get it as bad and so was able to care for the rest of us. He got his own meals, refilled sippy cups and bottles, changed diapers, and just kept us going. Our dining room table became our pharmacy with bottles of medicine all over it. None of us had any appetite and got our calories from Tylenol, Nyquil, ibuprofen, juice, Mucinex, cough syrup, and throat lozenges.

Times when we have multiple sick children, they just camp out in the living room. We bring out the blankets, pillows, and even buckets if they're needed. It's much easier than running up and down the stairs all night. The amazing thing is how a three-foot child can take up a whole five-foot couch with all his paraphernalia.

When we were sick with the influenza, our littlest tyke watched us taking temperatures so often that he began to try taking his own. He would get hold of the thermometer and try jabbing it under his arm. He would also go get his own Kleenex, blow his nose in it, and throw it in the trash. He must have realized that Mom was down for the count and he had to take over some things on his own. It's those little cute things that happen in the midst of sickness that keep you going until you're better. And remembering that it will pass. And before you know it, everyone is well again, and spring is in the air.

~~~~~~

Then there is the dreaded chickenpox. I am one of those moms who don't mind if her kids are exposed to chickenpox and even have the nasty thought of purposely exposing them just to get the disease over with.

We got the chickenpox in the middle of the summer that I was pregnant with kiddo number four. Our oldest son had already had them, so I only had two to get through it. I noticed the first spots on our second son when I laid him down for his nap one afternoon. He was scratching his belly, so I lifted his shirt and three or four big pox stared back at me. That's when your heart starts sliding to your toes, and you mentally begin ticking off all the things you had on your to-do list for the next week.

He didn't have a bad case at all. But his was just a drop in the bucket compared to our daughter. She came down with it exactly two weeks after our son. Now she truly had the chickenpox! Poor girl, she had it just about everywhere, from the top of her head to her fat little feet. In fact, one day I decided to try counting the spots—at least the ones I could see. So I began on the back of her leg, near her knee area.

By the time I had gotten to forty and had only moved a few inches on her body, I gave up the counting thing. She probably had several hundred on her. Some were even on her eyelids. She may have even had some in her mouth and throat because she gagged a few times and threw up, besides not eating enough to keep a mouse alive.

But we made it through, and it always seems as though there is something the little ones do that lets you know they are getting back to their normal selves.

It was five or so days later, and I was on the phone in the study. After about 10 minutes, I had the nagging thought that maybe I should check on the children. I found Megan sitting on top of the dining room table where I had stacks of cookbooks, *Taste of Home* magazines, and my recipe card box on the table, along with a tall glass of Pepsi. She had jerked out quite a few recipe cards, spilled my Pepsi on them and the magazines, and then proceeded to gleefully dump salt and pepper all over the sticky mess. Needless to say, I nearly hit the ceiling while trying to calmly hang up the phone without sounding too rude to the person on the other end.

But at least she was feeling well and being her ornery self once again—like taking apart cassette tapes, pitching dripping wet toys out of the tub, and pulling books off the shelves that I had put back just ten minutes earlier.

Yet, I'd still rather have an ornery child than a very sick one—although both tend to have the same outcome. Either way, you need a bucket and a rag.

Happiness is a state of mind.

"But He was wounded for our transgressions, He was bruised for our iniquities: the chastisement of our peace was upon Him; and with His stripes we are healed."

(Isaiah 53:5)

Sanity Tip: *When your children are sick, learn to set aside your work and take it easy for a few days. You will especially want to do this if you are sick with them. When we are all sick around here, we have a party. We get out our favorite books,* *videos, story tapes, blankets, and pillows, and we just hang out in the living room. If you need to lie around, you may as well have fun!*

Chapter 8

In the Ditch with Terrel

Wintertime here in the mountains of Idaho is gorgeous. Breathtakingly gorgeous. It amazes me how God can take a world that has turned so brown and dry from lack of rain for months and make it serenely beautiful with little flakes of snow. Watching the transformation that winter brings just reinforces my belief in an awesome Creator. All becomes still when the snowflakes are falling. Still enough that it seems as if you are the only person in the world.

When we get the first snow here in November or December, we celebrate by baking. Usually, we bake cinnamon rolls or some other such goodie. And once we have several inches on the ground, all the sleds come out and the children delight in sliding down our hill. What can be more fun than having Daddy slide you down a snowy hill? Usually, none of the children are ready to come in when Daddy is, though.

A mama is hard pressed to come up with things to keep four little munchkins busy during the winter months. Not every day is a good day to go sledding, especially when the hill ends on the road. We usually want an adult out there to help stop them before they reach the road. And so we have to come up with ideas for inside activities.

A huge blanket draped over two chairs makes a great tent where it's fun for them to eat a picnic consisting of a pea-nut-butter-and-jelly sandwich in a brown-paper lunch bag.

We bought two football helmets for a quarter each at a garage sale one summer, and they came in handy the following winter when two little boys liked to play football. One boy was the Jaguar's team and one was the Cheetah's team, or whatever name they could come up with. Masking tape works great for making a number on the backs of their shirts. And a number is a big deal for a miniature quarterback! One of my little guys also talked me into buying a set of small elbow and knee pads at a thrift store. They get used quite a bit for inside household stunts.

Another activity to keep little hands busy and little tummies full is to make them edible play dough. We have a recipe for peanut butter play dough, which makes a great mid-morning snack. Because we end up with dough on the chairs, all over the table, and on the floor, many times I limit play dough days to Thursdays, which is the day before cleaning day. Then it doesn't matter if they make a huge mess because it will get cleaned up within twenty-four hours anyway.

If the children are in scrap-booking moods, we dig through our pile of hunting and truck magazines to find the oldest issues. They cut out pictures, glue them on construction paper, add a sticker or two, write their name on it, punch holes in the side to put yarn through, and they have a real scrapbook to proudly show Daddy when he comes home.

For times when I have reached the limit of my sanity, am functioning on the last marble in my brain, or am clinging to the end of my rope, the bath is an awesome place for little bodies to wiggle around. It gives them a whole new environment, albeit a wet one. And, of course, you will probably end up with a flood all over the bathroom floor. But they will have had bundles of fun, will have gotten clean besides, and Mama will have had a few minutes of relative peace and quiet.

~~~~~~

One winter, we had a great time sledding with a family from church, although we did our sliding in the dark! It was in the dead of winter, and the sun had, probably smirkingly, set around 4:30. We were scheduled to go sledding at 7:00 p.m. Thankfully, the moon came to our rescue and shone brightly, plus some of us wore little headlamps over our sock hats.

The road we went sledding down is about a half mile from our house and goes up the mountain behind our house. It's just a dirt mountain road with winding curves and bears and cougars and steep drop-offs and … well, you can see why I became just a tad bit concerned when it was my turn to slide down. Actually, the drop-offs were not too steep—you'd just receive a nice headache from that tree you bumped into.

Ahh, yes, the trees. Have you ever noticed how many trees there are in the Rocky Mountains? Well, I had visions of veering off course, over the bank, and waking up to find myself wrapped around a giant evergreen.

Since you now know how crazy it might have seemed, let me tell you how it actually went. My first ride down was with Lowell on a runner sled. We were on our stomachs (that was so we could give that tree a kiss before it knocked us silly), and Lowell was steering it.

Now I didn't have any particular job to do except hang on for dear life and yell the whole way down. I was very good at my job, I might add. Except that my teeth got really cold from my mouth being open so much and freezing air rushing in. But have you ever tried to slide down a half mile of curves on your stomach in the dark and still keep your mouth shut? It was heaps of fun, and my sweet husband had the courtesy not to bury me in a snowbank.

Then they said it was my turn to try it by myself, and so they handed me a plastic sled. Now I was given instructions that, to turn a certain way, you're supposed to put a certain hand out in the snow and vice versa to turn the other way. I spent that whole half mile trying to remember which hand took me which way and you know, I still can't remember which hand does what. That's a blonde for you.

Terrel, our four-year-old, thought he was brave enough to try going with me, so we sent nearly everyone else ahead of us and hopped in our sled. We started whizzing down the mountain, when all of a sudden we found ourselves sitting in a snow bank! Well, I was sitting—Terrel was partially buried.

Since they had driven us all up the mountain, Lowell was still at the truck and came running down to get Terrel. I wanted to wipe the smirk off Lowell's face, but I refrained and gave Terrel to him to take to the truck. Poor little boy, I think it was a rather traumatic experience for him.

Lowell took Terrel to the truck, and I continued my journey on down. I pretty much took up the whole road with all my weaving back and forth, getting stuck in another snow bank, and having to start all over again. Lowell was in the truck with a few others who were following me down the mountain. He says I provided great entertainment for the ride down.

Oh well, you can't put a blonde on a sled a half a mile up in the air, in the dark, and expect her to come out with flying colors. All that came out was something flying—I think it was me. It really was great fun, and who knows, I may have had an audience in the woods, but with all of my shrieking, I'm sure I didn't hear them.

I will say that it was an experience of a lifetime, and perhaps we will try it again! When you have snow for five months out of the year, and you begin counting the snow in feet, not inches, then you finally decide the stuff is here to stay so you might as well have fun in it.

Life is not measured by the number of breaths we take but by the moments that take our breath away.

"As the hart panteth after the water brooks, so panteth my soul after Thee, O God." (Psalm 42:1)

Sanity Tip: *Here is my recipe for edible play dough. Mix 1 cup powdered sugar, ½ cup peanut butter, and ¼ cup honey. Hand it to your kids and walk away or you may be discouraged at the state of your table or kitchen.*

Chapter 9

Prayer I.V.

The house was quiet. So I knelt by my bed to begin my devotions. *Okay, Lord, I'm here. You know how much I want to spend time with You, to worship You, and to feel Your Spirit in the stillness....*

"Mom! The baby hit his head and he's crying really, really loud!"

Lord, I'll be right back. I promise, I'm coming back.

"Mom! Are you coming?"

Forgive me, Lord; it might not be within five minutes, but I'll meet up with You sometime today....

If you are a mom with toddlers, you know how extremely frustrating a personal devotional time can be. Interruptions can come every thirty seconds, and you leave your devotions feeling as dry as when you came. As this happens day after day, you find that your desire for fellowship with God begins to wane. You no longer feel close to Him, and, instead, you are now laden with guilt.

Guilt because you cannot seem to produce the desire to want to know Him among thirty-second interruptions. Guilt because you are so tired you don't want to get up thirty minutes earlier to meet with Him. Guilt because it seems as though no other moms have this same problem.

I'll give you a peek into my heart to let you know that you are not alone and also how I have learned to worship my Lord. And I will include a few other tips for you from other moms. I'm not saying that this is the only way to do it; these are just some ideas that have helped me through tough toddler years.

In the years before babies, I had a wonderful scheduled devotional time every morning with my Lord. It was where I met Him and took His presence with me throughout my day. After baby number one came along, that began to change. I was tired from waking up all hours of the night and soon found that

I had no desire to get up earlier. Babies two and three came along, and I was coping the best I knew how with devotions squeezed in whenever I could. But, still, I felt guilty.

Guilt hung over my devotional life because I did not feel that I met up with my expectations. I thought that, to be a good Christian, I had to have thirty to sixty minutes of time alone with God. I still did my devotions and still loved my Lord, but guilt was hounding my footsteps. Looking back, I sometimes wonder how much God enjoyed our times together when most of the time I came to Him out of guilt. It's sad, I know, but I don't believe I'm the only mom who has felt this way.

The way I viewed my devotional time with the Lord began to change when Lowell had his accident, which I'll cover in a later chapter. After he came home from the hospital, I had scarcely five minutes to myself, let alone sixty minutes. But I can say that I have never in my life felt as close to my Savior as I did then.

You're probably wondering how that can be when I could not spend my allotted quality time with God.

It's something I like to think of as my prayer I.V. We all know what an intravenous tube is. It is a tube that gives life-sustaining nutrition to a person totally dependent upon it.

That's exactly where I was. I was totally dependent upon the strength I received from my Lord. I drew from my intravenous tube of prayer every hour of every day. It connected me to Him, and, without it, I would have shriveled up and died inside.

I talked to Him while washing dishes. I cried out to Him while taking a shower. I prayed to my Lord in the middle of the night. I got short bursts of life-giving sustenance so many times throughout my day that I did not keep count.

But I felt alive! I felt close to my Lord. I was no longer coming out of guilt. Instead, I was coming out of desperation. And soon that desperation turned into a desire that has resulted in a love far deeper than I have ever known.

Since life is back to more of a normal routine, I now have longer than five minutes to spend with my Lord. But I will not give up my prayer I.V. It is my lifeline to heaven, and some days I'm on it all the time. It is the only way I can get through.

For you moms who struggle to keep your eyes open during Bible reading and your thoughts in a coherent line while praying, take courage. It will not always be like this. Someday, you will have had two nights in a row with eight hours of solid sleep, and you can enjoy your devotions.

But how do you get through these years of sleepless nights and interruptions all day long?

Begin by lowering your expectations. *I believe God wants quality time, not quantity time.* And if your quality time is five minutes here and there throughout the day, that is better than nothing at all.

A good friend once told me to remember that life is full of seasons. This is the summer season of your life where you are constantly busy serving other people's needs. Things will slow down a little later in the sense that you won't need to go change a diaper the moment you open your Bible. Later, you will have your hours to sit and worship Him. But for now, give Him the five or ten minutes throughout the day that you do have.

Some ladies like to put scripture verses on three-by-five cards and set them throughout the house where they can meditate on them during the day. I read a tip on keeping all of your devotional stuff together in a basket so it can be moved wherever you find yourself with five, ten, or twenty minutes to sit down.

And I discovered just the other day that, in addition to my prayer and Bible-reading, I truly *can* worship God while making supper, folding wash, or even scrubbing toilets. I put together two cds of some of my favorite Christian songs— songs that hold a special meaning to me or that help me to worship Him. I turned it on rather loud so I could hear it throughout the house, and I actually enjoyed my time cleaning toilets that day. I know that's a hard thought to wrap your mind around, but it can be done.

God is a spirit, and our spirits can connect with Him no matter where we are or what we're doing.

I'm not suggesting that we use our toddler and baby years as an excuse to give up our devotional time with Him. That's not what I mean at all. Instead, I want you moms to know that there is a way through these years where you can come out feeling full, satisfied, and in love with your Lord, rather than coming out feeling empty and dry as a bone.

It might take resetting your priorities to get it done, but it can be done. I like to make it a priority that the first book I sit down and read is my Bible. If I have time to sit down and read my *Taste of Home* magazine or that book I got at the library, then I *do* have time to read my Bible.

Give Him the best you can out of a heart of love and not guilt. He will, in turn, meet you with the sweetest presence you have ever known.

God can whisper at any minute of any day; we just need to be quiet and listen.

"The Lord hath heard my supplication; the Lord will receive my prayer." (Psalm 6:9)

Sanity Tip: *Reading Bible stories to your children is another way to worship Him and meditate on His Word. It also gives you the opportunity to teach your children what God has done in your life. Also, pray with your children, even for their small problems. Whether it's finding that toy they lost or praying for a friend who is hurt, they need to know that our God cares about the little things as well as the big.*

Chapter 10

A Typical Day

Have you ever wondered what someone else's day looks like? There are many days when I am at my wit's' end and would just love to know that I am not the only mom who gets a bit frazzled.

I'm sure we all know a "perfect family." The mother is up at 5:30 a.m. to make biscuits and gravy for her tribe while starting her bread dough for the day. By breakfast she has a load or two of laundry on the line. The children wake up in happy moods, and nobody pinches the other for beating him down the stairs. The father comes home from work in the evening with a huge grin on his face even though somebody had stolen a very expensive tool from his job site that day.

Then there are the rest of us moms who can barely drag ourselves out of bed by the time the children come tumbling down the stairs. Our bread dough is doing good to be in the mixing bowl before noon, and, as for biscuits and gravy, well, let's just say that we consider that a supper food around here— not breakfast. And, yes, the child who is the last one down the stairs has the tendency to show his displeasure to the winning sibling. As for laundry, well, sometimes it gets forgotten until the pile starts to resemble Mount Everest. And Daddy doesn't always come home with a huge grin on his face, although he tries. But sometimes I'm sure he would rather go right back to that job site, especially after he tries to walk through a maze of Legos, Tinker toys, train sets, sippy cups, and cookie crumbs. Oh, yeah, I forgot to vacuum that day.

Now here is where I will tell you a little secret. These "perfect families" do not exist—at least not down here on earth anyway. Nobody can be perfect all the time. Some of us can't even manage it for five minutes! Every family has its good times and its bad times. Nobody is perfect.

We are all differently dysfunctional. Once we accept that, we can begin to enjoy our children and raise them the best we know how. All God asks is that we love Him with all our hearts and do our utmost to love our children and raise them in His ways.

So I will venture to open the door to my home a bit here and give you a typical day in our lives. I said *typical* because every day brings a new challenge and new adventure. In fact, just writing this book has been a challenge with four kiddos around.

6:00 a.m. "Mama!" My gritty eyes open to see what time it is. "Mama!!" I pull the covers up a bit more, hoping Logan, our two-year-old, will go back to sleep. "Maamaaa!" Maybe if I wait a few more seconds Lowell will take pity on me and go get him. "Maaamaaa!" All right, all right, I'm coming, you flesh-and-blood alarm clock. I wish I could reset him to wake up at 7:00. No such luck; so, instead, I bring him downstairs with me and change his diaper, which, by the way,

I'm getting pretty good at doing with my eyes half closed. "Ina get in bed wich you," he says sweetly. Great! I'm all for getting back into my nice warm bed for a while yet.

So back into bed we go to snuggle a bit. "Scoot ober, please," he says rather demandingly. He is two years old and weighs about twenty-six pounds but still thinks he needs about half of our queen-size bed. Spoiled, I know. And I'm such a softie, especially when it comes to snuggling with my babies in a big, warm, soft bed. Now all we have to do is wait for the four-year-old to come join us.

After telling secrets for a while and getting lots of kisses, we hear footsteps outside the door. Megan has arrived to join the party! So now there are three of us in bed telling secrets and giving kisses. And if it's a Saturday, that means Daddy is still in bed with us. That is when it gets really interesting! We all fight for who gets to snuggle next to Dad. But by the time the body count reaches five or six in our bed, I'm out of there. I have had my share of toes, knees, and elbows in my back to last me for the day, thank you very much.

I step out into the hall to make my way to the coffee pot and almost get run over by the two oldest boys as they come racing down the stairs. Now I don't know where they get that much energy in the morning, but it tends to sound as though a thundering herd of elephants lives on the floor above us. I'm safer just to let the herd pass me by and then make my own slow way to the coffee corner of our kitchen.

So now the coffee's perking, and I'm headed back up to get dressed, when I glance in my room at what used to be my bed. There are two big lumps that have the quilt wrapped around them, just waiting for me to tickle them. So I unwrap one lump to find Megan inside, and by the time I reach for the second lump, it pops out to say, "Here I am!" Logan has no patience whatsoever, especially when hiding from someone.

Once we all have clean clothes on and our hair is combed, we head to the kitchen for breakfast. Actually, I'll have to tell you another secret. Sometimes my darling daughter, Megan, doesn't get her hair combed until 9:00, 10:00, or even until the next day! Shameful, I know. But her hair can be a tad intimidating to comb, especially first thing in the morning and before I've had my coffee. Her hair is a mass of curls, and after sleeping on it all night, she can look very scary.

Now where were we? Oh, yeah, breakfast. I've got another awful secret. A few days of the week, my children pretty much get their own breakfast. Hey, I warned you I'm not perfect! So don't sit there with your mouth hanging open, please. The older boys get out the cold cereal, bowls, spoons, and milk. If one of them wants homemade yogurt, they can get it from the 'fridge. Other days, we have eggs and toast. But don't even mention pancakes or waffles, because that is either a Saturday breakfast or a supper food around here, just like biscuits and gravy are.

After breakfast is chore time. Derek, our seven-year-old, is in charge of the animals. So he runs off to feed and water the dog and cat. Terrel, five, and Megan, four, get to empty the dishwasher. Logan, two, tries to help but mostly just gets in the way.

Once the dishwasher is emptied, the dirty clothes need to be thrown down from upstairs. Have you ever seen those houses with laundry chutes? Well I've got four of them. They are ages two through seven, and they have fun wadding their dirty clothes into balls and throwing them down the stairway, trying to make them land in the laundry basket at the bottom. I know that's not the traditional way of getting the dirty laundry from upstairs, but, hey, it works for us. Besides, I don't think we're quite normal around here anyway.

Chores are done, and now it is time for school for the two oldest boys. We are homeschooling Derek, who is in first grade, and Terrel, who is in kindergarten. Megan is in sticker class and Logan is in Crayola grade. We sit down at the kitchen table and get out our schoolbooks. If the two littlest cannot be quiet enough, we send them to the basement to watch Winnie the Pooh. He's quite educational, right?!

School usually takes us about an hour, which is just the right amount of time for me to get my morning cup of coffee consumed. After school, the children can play inside until it warms up a bit. Then they like to go play in the snow.

Lunch can consist of anything from peanut-butter-and-jelly sandwiches to hot dogs to leftovers. If it's summer, I like to pack them a picnic lunch and send them outside to eat. It keeps the mess out of my house and gives them a fun activity.

After lunch is nap time. Right now, we have only one consistent napper in the bunch, but the others are required to have quiet time. They must leave me alone for an hour and find something quiet to do.

This is my sanity time. If I've had a harrowing day, it helps to get me through it if I know I will have an hour to sit by myself somewhere quiet or even take a nap. I firmly believe that every mother must have something she can do to help preserve her sanity. Yours may be to take a walk, take a long bath, have a hot cup of tea, or whatever. Mine is to sit somewhere quiet, whether it's at the computer or reading a book or having my devotional time. If I have a cup of hot tea, it's even better. And if I have a piece of chocolate, I'll come away with my sanity completely intact!

Don't feel guilty about taking some time away from the dishes, diapers, and dirty clothes to have a few minutes for yourself. Think of it this way—it also preserves your husband's and children's sanity. Because you've all heard the saying, "If mama ain't happy, ain't nobody happy." A happy wife makes a happy husband, and a happy mama makes for happier kids. So the next time your husband comes home to find you sitting in a tub full of bubbles at 2:00 in the afternoon, tell him you are doing it to keep him happy! Just don't let him reply to that one.

It's now 3:00, and the nappers are awake and raring to go once again. Now that my sanity has been restored, I must start thinking about supper. Daddy usually arrives home around

5 or 6 and we eat soon afterwards. After supper, we try to spend some time together as a family. The children, even our daughter, Megan, love to wrestle with Daddy. He can have all four of them caught and will not let go until they cry, "Uncle!" I sit and watch and, once in a while, get into the midst of the fray myself. But usually I just provide a soft place for a child to land after they escape from Daddy's clutches. There's nothing quite like getting your back put into place by having four kiddos land on it.

By the time someone has really bunged up his elbow, knee, back, or head pretty good, it's time to get out the Bible-story book. After reading our Bible story for the evening, who-ever wants to can say a little prayer. Even two-year-old Logan likes to whisper everybody's names before closing with a hasty amen.

Then it's a race to get a snack, teeth brushed, pottied up, and pajamas on. After they are all in bed, the day still isn't over. Not until there is no noise coming from the two bedrooms upstairs do I relax enough to go to sleep. Instead, Lowell and I like to read while sharing a bag of Twizzlers. We take turns going upstairs when the noise level warns us that a party is starting. We haven't had to resort to flipping coins to see whose turn it is to be referee, but that's not to say it won't happen in the future.

I went upstairs one time to find both Megan's and Logan's beds empty. I heard a snicker underneath Logan's daybed, and sure enough, I bent over to find four big round eyes looking up at me.

Another time, I walked into their room to find the beds empty. The closet light was on and the doors partially shut. They must have thought they were being sneaky by trying to close their closet doors from the inside. I guess they figured my hearing was bad, too, because I heard some mighty loud whispers coming from inside that closet. I opened the doors to find them sitting on top of an old dresser I keep in the closet.

They'd been caught red-handed and they sure knew it! Needless to say, that night was pretty quiet from then on.

Well, that about sums up a typical day here. Of course, I didn't tell you of the time Megan fell and busted her lip. Nor of how I shut myself in the office just so I could have a quiet phone conversation. And then there was that diaper of Logan's that took the award as Diaper of the Year.

I also didn't mention the days that I stand in the kitchen at 5:00 p.m., not knowing what I'm going to make for dinner, and so get out a frozen pizza instead. But I realize as I'm getting the pizza that the littlest guy had found the temperature knob on the freezer to be interesting and had turned my freezer off 24 hours ago.

Or the day that, had you been peeking, you would have seen me on my hands and knees scrounging for that last special sippy cup. You know, the favorite one that your toddler throws someplace and you cannot find it for days. Then when you do find it, it looks as though someone barfed in it and smells even worse.

And the times that poor Daddy comes home from work so tired, and the kids are getting on his nerves, so you have to banish them to the basement. Then he realizes that one of the children turned off his computer that day and messed up some stuff. And to top it all off, you sit your family down to that frozen pizza that you accidentally left a little too long in the oven.

Then you all join hands and thank the Lord for this day and this burned pizza.

Ever have days like those, where nothing seems to go right and everything seems to go wrong? I have a tip for you.

Laugh.

You may not be able to laugh right then, but tell yourself you will laugh at this later. Find the humor in it and be thankful that you have another day to hug that ornery two-year-old who flushed his race car down the toilet. Proverbs 17:22

says, "A merry heart doeth good like a medicine...." So take your medicine and smile, Mama!

Children are with us but a few passing years—our unending list of things to get done will be with us even when the children are out the door.

"Children's children are the crown of old men; and the glory of children are their fathers." (Proverbs 17:6)

Sanity Tip: *Throw your to-do list out the window. On an especially hectic day, lock yourself in the bathroom or bedroom for ten minutes to have a cup of hot coffee or to talk on the phone to another adult. Just make sure the children know to come get you if somebody is seriously injured!*

Chapter 11

Water, Sand, and Cows

Summertime in the mountains has a celebratory air. Since winters can be so long, it seems as if everything is throwing a big party all summer long. People live outside, and there is some rodeo, fair, or parade going on every Saturday, not to mention all the garage sales on Friday. Not only do the people celebrate, but the animals do, too. Prairie dogs buzz around as though living on Mountain Dew, bears scare the dickens out of blueberry pickers, and deer go to town nibbling on all the tender plants they can find … including my garden.

Children also relish in the warm summer sunshine. Boots, coats, and hats get traded for swimming trunks. My kids love to play in their little wading pool. I have to fill up the pool in the morning so that by afternoon it is warm since the mountain water here is so frigid it would turn you into a giant popsicle.

And as the water is heating up, the pool gets used as a fishing hole. The kids get a long stick, have me tie a string on the end, and go fishing. Usually there is some kind of bait attached to the string. This can be anything from a truck to a dinosaur. The pool also gets all kinds of odd items thrown in it: rocks, balls, trucks, even a spoon or two from my utensil drawer.

Besides the pool, we have a sandbox that has seen many hours of children playing happily in it, although there are some rather unhappy moments if you count the few piercing screams I've heard. The children seem to think sand has health benefits when applied to the head, face, eyes, and ears.

One summer, our seventeen-month-old Megan was sitting outside in the dirt when I looked out the window to see her two-and-a-half-year-old brother calmly dumping spoonsful of sand on her head. I heard a scream, but when it subsided I realized it had been me. Megan had taken it better than I had. She didn't seem too perturbed at her brother, or, perhaps, she was quietly planning her revenge.…

The following summer, we had a new baby in the house, another guy a little lower on the totem pole than Megan. She used this to her advantage one summer day as the seven-month-old baby was sitting in the sandbox. Quite calmly, she began dumping sand on his nearly-bald head and delightedly watched as it slid down around his ears to settle in the crevices of his coat and clothes. The little trooper didn't yell either. He just sat there watching that funny-looking stuff trickle off his forehead to land on his belly. The moral of the story is that life comes full circle, and you don't want to be the lowest one on the totem pole.

~~~~~~

Most years, we have a garden in which to grow some fresh vegetables for freezing and canning and just plain eating.

The kids love to help plant it, pick it, and eat it. They have even helped me weed it a little—precious little. But every little weed pulled helps.

Speaking of little, I told Terrel to go out one day and get me some zucchini for a stir-fry. He was so very proud to go pick some all by himself. After a while, he came back in with a handful of zucchini.

Now picture how big a four-year-old's hand is, and you will know how much zucchini he brought me. He had found some of the smallest zucchinis I have ever beheld. In fact, had I been picking them, at first glance I would have thought them yellow and green worms. You know, the kind that live on your tomato bushes. But I thanked him just the same for his hard work and threw those few bites of zucchini in the pan.

One summer I gave each of the three oldest children a pack of seeds to plant in our salad spot. We had one corner of the garden in which to plant lettuce, spinach, and radishes.

They were thrilled to be planting their own garden. So they put the seeds in the ground, and we covered them up with a little dirt. Then almost every day after that, they would check on them to see if they were growing yet. To them, it seemed to take forever until they found a little green leaf sticking above the dirt.

When it was time to harvest peas, we all had a grand time pulling the pea pods off the vine. But I had to pretty much shell the peas myself, although they liked to eat the freshly shelled peas in my bowl.

Our garden has some very good memories in it and a few not so good ones, too. One summer we had some uninvited visitors to our little land of vegetables. One Sunday morning, we were all sleeping away until around 4:30 a.m. Lowell and I heard some cows mooing quite near our windows. Lowell actually heard them walking—he's such a light sleeper. I was still somewhere between reality and dreamland, so what I heard

was this incessant mooing getting closer to my ear. All I wanted was for them to *please shut up* and let me go back to sleep!

Lowell got up and stuck his head out the window to see
cows trotting through our yard. He ran out onto the porch and
discovered that they were munching away on my flowers and
stomping through my garden! He threw some stones at them to
get them back down the road to their pasture and then called
the owners.

To this day, I'm still not sure if the cows hightailed it
home because of the stones he threw or because of what Lowell
looked like in his sleepwear. Anyway, the owners of the cows
came out and supposedly fixed the fence.

Monday I went out to my precious garden and tried to
prop up my sweet corn that I'm sure was midget-size compared
to an Indiana farmer's corn. But I got it all nicely weeded and
propped back up.

After supper, Lowell and I took the children for a bike
ride to the neighbors. As we were talking to them, we heard

that same crazy mooing as though the cows were especially delighted with themselves. We jumped on our bikes, hoped all the kids had gotten in the bike cart, and raced home. As we got closer home, we could see that the cows had indeed returned. Six to eight of them were gorging themselves on my potato and corn plants.

We started yelling like a couple Indians to scare them away. They ran away all right—right over my corn, which they had been scrumptiously munching, stomped all over my potatoes, squashed a little broccoli, and charged through the pea fence, even going so far as tipping over a railroad tie. I think right then I could've strangled a cow and had it ground into hamburger before another "moo" could be uttered. Needless to say, I was really having to work on a Christ-like spirit.

And yet that isn't the end of the story. As the cows were hastily exiting our garden, one of them topped it all off by leaving afresh, huge cow patty right smack in the middle of the pathway.

The next day, I was trying to pick a few precious peas with my two little helpers when Megan came through the garden calmly carrying her little kitten. Completely oblivious to anything, as every true blonde should be, she stuck her dainty little foot right in that manure pile. And don't ask me how, but *somehow* it managed to get on her dress, up her legs, and on her hands.

That's when I would've gladly gone back to bed and started the week all over again. But a mom can't do that, so we took her to the shower and scrubbed her down. With every whiff of her, I was having to adjust my attitude once again. I guess the Lord took one of His most humble creatures to teach me some much-needed lessons. Just don't go offering me a quarter-pounder with cheese anytime soon ... I could get rather violent.

Don't cry because it's over; smile because it happened.

"Then our mouth was filled with laughter, and our tongue with singing. The Lord has done great things for us, and we are glad." (Psalm 126:2a–3)

Sanity Tip: *Let the little ones help plant, pick, and pull. A garden is a place for them to learn how amazing our God truly is. Besides, who cares if your rows aren't evenly spaced and a bean plant gets mistaken for a weed?*

Chapter 12

I Gotta Go!

When you have four children in five years, you will inevitably have diaper troubles. There will be many days you wish you could turn their valves off so you do not have to look at one more soggy, dripping diaper or wipe up one more mess. But that just doesn't happen. Besides, if it did, we'd have a fatal problem on our hands. So try to remember that the next time you get done changing a two-month-old's poopy diaper and realize with utter disgust that there is a green tinge under your fingernails.

Our firstborn was only a few weeks old when I got a foreshadow of things to come in the next two decades. I had him lying on the changing table, which was in a corner of the room, so there were walls on two sides of it. His head was pointed toward the room and his hind end toward the wall. I took off his diaper and proceeded to get a new one. I heard a grunt and watched in absolute horror as a volcano of yellow poo erupted from my little angel. It hit the wall and began to slide down, leaving an orange path in its wake! I had never seen anything like it, nor have I since.

I'm sure you moms have all had times when you caught yellow goo peeking out at you from the edges of your dolly's diaper. Then there are the times it comes completely through and up the back of your little munchkin.

There was one such time when our oldest was a few month's old and we were preparing to go to church. We got all dressed up in our Sunday finest. I was wearing a solid cream dress. Now for you first-time moms, I have one really good piece of advice: *Never wear a solid white or cream dress. Ever.* At least not until your baby has been potty trained, or maybe even sent to school, or perhaps wait until he has even married.

I was about to learn this lesson in a most grotesque manner. My precious boy was sitting on my lap, happily lick-ing his chops from his middle-of-the-sermon snack while we were sitting in the nursery. For those of you who have never heard a newborn's eruptions, that's exactly what it sounds like. An eruption. As though someone shook a bottle of pop and then opened the lid. Sometimes it keeps coming and coming, and there's no way that little diaper covering your baby's buns can even begin to hold it in. So it must find somewhere else to go. And that is usually *out*. Up the back, through the sides, and down the legs.

By this time, I was getting used to these eruptions and would just let him finish his job before changing him into a clean one. We moms know that a baby takes perverse delight in pooping into a clean diaper the minute you put it on him, if not thirty seconds after. So I calmly let him finish and then picked him up to take him over to the changing table. It's a wonder my gasp of horror was not heard throughout the entire church as I gazed in abject misery at the yellow mess all over the skirt of my pretty cream dress. Had my dress been a darker color, it might not have shown up as bad. But as it was, my dress was nearly white and showed the entire stain.

There was no way I was going back into church with poop all over my skirt, so I had another mom go tell my husband I needed him. We left church before it was ended so I could save my pride a bit.

I will tell you moms one good thing about changing so many diapers every day, all day, for years on end. You can almost do it in your sleep. In fact, you don't even need much light since you begin to develop a sixth sense, such as a blind person does. The diapers, wipes, and baby parts are all where they were yesterday, unless someone swapped your girl baby for a boy baby in the night. Your mind and your hands go on automatic, and you' find yourself waking up to find a dirty diaper sitting on your nightstand or you step on it when getting out of bed in the morning and wonder how it got there in the first place. Just don't be surprised sometime if you find one sitting in your 'fridge because you accidentally mistook the 'fridge for the trash can at 2 a.m.

There does finally come a time in your young child's life when he will want to get out of those diapers. I know we all think it's never going to happen, but Lowell always assures me that he hasn't yet seen diapers on a high school freshman.

It's now time for potty training, Mom. Get out your mop, rags, M&M's, and a bucketful of patience. You will need it.

Oh, and get your earplugs. You will also inevitably need those because sometime, somewhere, you will hear a story from a mom whose child was potty trained at one year old. Or from the mom whose toddler was potty trained in a day. Ignore these stories unless, of course, you are that mom. I mean no offense to these superwomen. I just know that they are few and far between. And I'm not one of them.

My children have a small amount of brain damage. The wiring that runs from their plumbing below to their brains up above is not fully connected until they are almost three years old. You must believe me that this is true. All three of them who are potty trained today were the same in this area, and I don't expect the fourth to turn over a new leaf in this family. He is a few months over two and despises his potty chair with a dislike that equals my abhorrence for all things reptile.

With our first child, I was going to be the perfect mom and have my child trained by two years old. I know I can hear you laughing. That was one whole year of complete torture for both Derek, my potty trainee, and me. I cajoled, I prodded, I even bribed. Nothing worked. One day he'd do wonderful. The next day I was wondering if I could renegotiate on my contract as a mom.

Somewhere around his third birthday, the Lord mercifully connected that wire that ran from his plumbing to his brain. Within a matter of days, he was potty trained.

Our second son came along and, being the competitive little guy that he is, decided at two years old that he could do what his older brother, Derek, did, including going to the potty.

Now he's always been a little short on one end and that was catastrophic while going potty. Even with a step stool, we still ended up with potty everywhere but in the toilet. An inch or two on his frame has done wonders in that area.

Even though he started potty training at two years old, he still wasn't fully trained until three years old. But he was the quickest of any of them yet.

Our little curly, blonde girl came along next. Now she has always been a bit behind the others in baby milestones. She sat at eight months, crawled at eighteen and a half months, and walked at twenty-one months, so I didn't even begin to potty train her until she had reached her third birthday. And by then there were moments that told me it was nearing the time to start.

One such embarrassing time was at church one Wednesday evening. We were all standing around talking, and I had put Megan down to play and wasn't watching where she was going. She was eighteen months old at the time and wasn't even crawling yet. She was our late crawler and walker. Instead, she would scoot. She scooted everywhere, inside and out.

Well before I knew it, a group of ladies was standing in the back laughing. Someone asked me, "Did you know Megan lost her diaper?" In horror, I turned to see Megan come scooting down the middle aisle right through a pack of men with nothing covering her behind and her dress creeping up around her waist.

Needless to say, I scooped her up, tried to hide my very red face, and headed to the nursery while I left Lowell to find the offending diaper. Someone said she made history with that one! All I know was that I wanted to climb under a bench about then. Of course, I was about seven months pregnant and would have probably gotten stuck.

Another incident that suggested the diaper days needed to be over was a day we were all at the library. As we were walking out to the van, the boys and I were a little faster at the walking thing than Megan and Lowell. Lowell says they were strolling along when he noticed that Megan was taking her good old time. He started pulling her by the hand, but she still wasn't hurrying up any. It seems she was doing more of a waddle than anything else. They were passing a lady sitting on a bench when the lady says, "Her diaper fell down!" Aghast, Lowell looked down at Megan only to behold her diaper had made its way below her knees and was creeping up on her ankles. Quickly he scooped her up, diaper and all, and whisked her to the privacy of the van. She certainly had a real thing for losing her diapers in public.

Now after reading this chapter, you have probably detected that potty training is one of my least favorite jobs in parenting. In fact, I downright dread it. Days of mopping up puddles all over the house, washing out underwear again and again, and making sure there is a bathroom everywhere we go. We have cause for a celebration when we do not have a potty trainee in the group.

So far right now we have one more toddler to train. Problem is, I can't remember where I left that bucketful of patience.…

When you get to your wits' end, you'll find God lives there.

"Peace I leave with you, my peace I give unto you: not as the world giveth, give I unto you. Let not your heart be troubled, neither let it be afraid." (John 14:27)

Sanity Tip: *Relax. Potty training can be one of the most stressful chores of parenting, so take a deep breath and remember* *that it will happen in its own time. When you've wiped up the fifth puddle for the day, tell yourself that this is such a small phase in your life, and that when you turn seventy, you will no longer remember it!*

Chapter 13

Kiddo Kapers

When our second son was born, our first little guy was twenty months old. He was still learning how to eat with a fork and spoon and many times made a huge mess. He was also a slow eater.

One Sunday morning, we were getting ready to go to church and I had made some scrambled eggs. Lowell and I were finished eating, and Derek was still in his high chair, taking his good, old time at swallowing his food.

He had a small pile of eggs waiting to be eaten, so I pushed them all on his fork. It was only one bite left, but it was a big bite! I left the room, thinking he'd feed himself. He put the bite in his mouth, trying to chew his way around the huge mouthful of eggs.

Now all of our children have an extremely sensitive gag reflex. If something is the least bit stringy or of a weird consistency, they will gag and sometimes throw up. Lowell was sitting there recording the little guy on video camera as he chewed. It wasn't exactly a chew, more just pushing it around in his mouth.

His face kept looking sicker and sicker as though he was full up to his ears and could not get this last bite swallowed. All of a sudden, he'd had enough, and up it all came! Of course, Daddy thought it was the funniest thing to get on video. But I'm not so sure that Derek will think it's funny once he reaches his teenage years.

~~~~~~

One summer when we still lived in Indiana, I was so excited to start my garden. We went to the greenhouse down the road and bought our broccoli plants, tomato plants, and seeds. We only had three children at the time, ages three, one and a half, and four months.

A couple mornings after we had put the little broccoli plants in their holes for the summer, I went out to the garden to find quite a surprise. My cute little plants were sitting quite neatly next to their holes, all dried out and shriveled up! I thought perhaps an animal had dug them up, but there was no sign of digging. It seems my two little helpers had thought they were being quite the gardeners the day before and had calmly pulled my plants out of their holes to lay them on the ground.

~~~~~~

I like to take my kiddos with me most places and most times, although a few times I've come back home thinking it would have been better all around to have found a babysitter. One such time that remains in my memory was when we went blueberry picking. This was something I had been looking for-ward to since the beginning of May. Time can seem to crawl by when you are anticipating an event for months, but it was finally here.

In my planning and preparation, I pictured the children delightfully helping Lowell and me pick these scrumptious blueberries. They would be quite well behaved while dropping the berries carefully in their buckets. There would be no fussing, no squabbling, and no hitting the sibling blocking their way, standing on their toes, or picking from their bush. And, of course, the sun would be shining gorgeously over the mountains, and all the mosquitoes would be busy tormenting other blueberry pickers in some other blueberry patch somewhere far away.

Well … you guessed it. Reality can hit hard. I had not counted on having to watch for snakes in the weeds nor how squished the berries can look after four little hands are done with them. Nor had I counted on the outhouse being so far away.

As I said, reality can hit hard. And it hit three-year-old Terrel about twenty minutes into picking time. I was trying, very greedily, to plop as many blueberries as I could in my bucket when I heard him yelling, "I gotta go stinky!"

I could tell from the panicked tone of his voice and the fact that he was standing with his legs spread apart that, yep, it had already happened. Now what are the chances that he would have a case of diarrhea right there in the blueberry patch? Chance or no, I hauled him to the van and cleaned him up. It had gotten on the insides of his britches, and considering that I don't usually take a change of clothes along for all members of our family, I had no pants to put on him.

So he was pantless for the last half hour. He was a little trooper, though. I was rather glad for the weeds that came up to his little belly. At least the other blueberry pickers couldn't see his bare legs and wonder exactly what kind of family they were picking alongside of.

After getting him cleaned up, we headed back to the patch, and before long, I had to carry Megan. Considering all the whining and fussing coming from her direction, I could tell she wasn't exactly thrilled with sitting in Daddy's backpack carrier. When it was all said and done, Lowell and five-year-old Derek were the ones who really picked the blueberries. And did they ever pick! They got 32 pounds in about 45 minutes! After that escapade, I'm wondering if it wouldn't be smartest to send those two out to the patch the next time the blueberries are ripe and ready.

And I'll stay at home sipping my iced tea until I hear someone yell, "Mom, I gotta go!"

I must also confess that my children can really humble me if given the chance. Or maybe it was my own stupidity that caused this incident. We were trying to get our vehicle titles changed over for Idaho plates after we had moved from Indiana the previous year. Lowell told me I needed to go into the courthouse and sign some papers for it, so before I could forget what he had told me to do and where to go, I packed all the children in the van and headed to town.

We parked at Safeway and walked across the street to a big old building. It looked like it should have been a courthouse—how was I to know that I was supposed to read signs? So we went charging inside, and I stood there a minute trying to figure out why this looked so familiar—rather like the post office.

I probably looked as blonde as they come because when I asked an elderly gentleman if this was the courthouse, he looked at me as though I had asked him if this was the White House. He kindly told me that it was the Post Office and pointed across the street to another old building, which was the courthouse. I tried to save what little dignity I had left by saying that we had just moved here. I could tell he didn't believe me.

Once I got outside with my brood, I looked up at the building, and wouldn't you guess, it said "Post Office." Feeling very sheepish, I guided my munchkins, barefoot no less, back across the street to the courthouse. Just as we mounted the steps to enter, I breathed a sigh of relief and told the children to go inside. Five-year-old Derek paused a couple seconds, looked at me, and said, "Are you *sure* this is the courthouse?"

After I picked my jaw up off the sidewalk, I had to tell myself I didn't blame him for doubting. But I did have to look at him twice to see if he was fourteen rather than four.

Children sure have a way of keeping life interesting.

~~~~~~

Lowell was headed out the door one Wednesday evening for a men's meeting at church when I told the boys to go get their pajamas on. So they got dressed and brushed their teeth. Since Derek had been at the dentist a couple months before and they had found cavities, the boys had been taking a fluoride prescription.

Now for those of you who have never seen a fluoride pill, it is a pill that practically begs kids to eat it. They are a perfect, tiny, kid-sized pill. And they are sweet. So you can imagine where this story is going.

When the boys were done brushing their teeth, Derek told me he had also taken his fluoride pill. That meant he had to have opened the bottle himself. So much for childproof bottles.

It wasn't two minutes later that Terrel came in the kitchen with the actual fluoride bottle itself and proudly handed it to me. "Mom, look what I did!" he said. In horror, I looked and behold, the whole bottle of pills was empty! Now to begin with, there were 90 of them little buggers in there. But they had used some up over the past couple months, and it was down to probably thirty. I asked him if he ate *all* of them, to which he promptly said, "Yes."

So I panicked. I sat Logan down on the kitchen floor and ran for the phone to call Lowell. Poor man, he'd only been out of the house five minutes before his scatterbrained wife had to call him. Lowell told me to call his mom. As I' was calling, I asked Terrel again where the pills were, just to see if he actually did eat them. He looked down at his little belly sticking out and then up at me as though he didn't know if I knew where food went when we ate it!

Well, when I got off the phone with Lowell, I heard Logan crying. I had a sinking feeling that I knew where I'd find him. I ran out to the living room to see him crying at the bottom of the basement stairs! In my panicked state, I had forgotten to close the gate to the stairs and my roly-poly munchkin had done a tumble bumble all the way down. It was carpeted, so he received a rug burn and a good-sized bump on his forehead.

Now I was really feeling like a horrible mom, and I had to go call my mother-in-law. So I did and she said to call poison control. Ugh. I was hoping I wouldn't have to do that. That's the number that *other* moms have to call when their *bad, bad* children drink bleach or toilet bowl cleaner, right?

But I swallowed my pride and dialed the number. The man who answered was very kind when I explained the situation to him. He said they get calls like that all the time and something about fluoride pills tasting sweet so little kids love to eat them. I told him that "Yea, I know. I ate a bunch one time when I was a kid." Then was when he laughed and said his mom always told him that life would come back to bite you.

Talk about humble pie! He said that Terrel could have eaten ten times that amount before they would've said to send him to ER. So he said to give him milk and he should be fine, which I did. I made Terrel open up and poured in a whole gallon of it! Actually, I only gave him a cupful. But I was so rattled that I think my dear husband wondered about me there for a while.

To calm myself, I decided to take a relaxing shower and go off duty for five minutes. I told Derek he was in charge. He wanted to know what "in charge" meant. I told him it meant he was the boss. His little eyes lit up. "Good!" he said.

It wasn't two minutes later that Derek came in to say that Terrel (yes, that little rascal again) was squirting something up his nose. Sighing, I told Derek to bring it to me. It was the decongestant drops I had sitting out for Logan's stuffy nose. When Lowell got home, I told him our kids were poppin' pills and snortin' drugs.

One catastrophic afternoon began this way. I knew that Megan and Logan were playing in my walk-in closet where we keep the changing table. Sometimes they like to play hide-and-seek in there. Soon I heard Logan cry a couple of times. I thought, *Oh, no, Megan's hurting him!*

As it turned out, she *was* hurting him, but in her two-year-old mind, she must have thought she was playing house with a live dolly because I opened the closet door to find both of them sitting in a pile of Vaseline. I'd had about a third of a good-sized can of the greasy stuff sitting on the changing table.

Megan had proceeded to smear it all over her hands and up her arms, on her dress, on the wall, and on the carpet. As if that wasn't enough, she had applied it quite lovingly, I'm sure, to Logan's head and clothes. Perhaps thinking it a facial cream, she had plopped loads of it on his eyes, which he tried in vain to wipe off. That only caused it to get smeared even more, including all over the back of the closet door.

The poor little tyke! His hair was a mass of grease, as were his eyelids. I quickly plunked him in the tub full of soapy water. Then the "little lady" got properly disciplined before getting plunked in the tub as well. When I tried to shampoo

Logan's hair, it didn't do a whole lot except smear the Vaseline around. So he was a regular grease monkey, thanks to his big sister. As for her, she was promptly put in bed following the bath. I didn't figure she could be too much ornerier while sleeping.

~~~~~~

One day, I was in the kitchen, and I put Logan, our one-year-old, in the sink so that I could do some work in the kitchen without holding him. Our sink is deep and has worked wonders when I've had a fussy one who wants to be right in the middle of what I'm doing. If I sit him on the counter, he might fall off, so the sink is one of the best placesuntil he learns to crawl out of it. It has been so much fun to watch other ladies' faces when they are at my home and I plop Logan in the sink to play. I go on with my work, and they always start gasping and laughing. I don't know if they think I'm going to give him a bath in the middle of Sunday dinner or what.

Well, this particular day, I was also talking on the phone while Logan was in the sink. I gave three-year-old Megan the job of entertaining him while I made a phone call. Now I don't know about you ladies, but my children automatically start their antics the minute I dial a phone number or the phone begins to ring. It must be an instinct this younger generation is born with. They just seem to know that, when Mommy or Daddy are on some electronic gadget, they can try to do what they want. You notice I said try.

There have been a few times that I've had to cut my telephone conversations extremely short so I could administer some discipline to my little band of angels.

I walked around the corner to better hear the other person on the phone, when all of a sudden, Logan began wailing a most pathetic wail. There are certain cries that need attention immediately, and this was one of them. I cut off the conversation and went back out to the kitchen where Logan was sobbing his heart out.

When I saw what was causing the crying, I had to go back around the corner to stifle my laughter before rescuing him. Megan had gotten hold of the hose sprayer attached to the sink, turned the water on, and was spraying Logan right in the face. She thought it was hilarious, especially while he was yelling! He was drenched from the top of his head down to his knees. I quickly got the poor darling out of harm's way, dried him off, and then, once again, took care of his ornery sister.

~~~~~~

Have you ever had one of those times when you thought you lost your child? You've called his name for ten minutes with no answer. You've looked upstairs, downstairs, under the beds, in the closets, and even in the shower, to no avail. Your heart is pounding, your hands are sweaty, and you feel on the verge of panicking. Finally, you find the little munchikin in a place you had overlooked and there he is with a huge grin on his face. Then is when you either fall over unconscious because your panic left so very suddenly and took your breath with it, or you crush the child in a hug that nearly smothers the poor thing.

Those times always make me feel so guilty, although I know every mom has them. We have to realize that only God can keep an eye on our children twenty-four hours a day, seven days a week. For us, we're human. And humans mess up once in a while.

There will be that one minute that you go get the dirty laundry from upstairs and you come down to find your child eating the laundry soap you'd been putting in the washer. Or the five minutes you were on the phone in the office and came back in the kitchen to see that your two-year-old had pushed a kitchen chair up to the silverware drawer and was helping himself to a newly-sharpened knife.

One fine summer day, I was talking on the phone with a good friend and was also trying to keep watch over my two littlest who were playing outside with the two oldest. Before long, the two oldest came in and found something else to do. I told them to go back outside and get the two little ones. So they ran back outside and tried to drag the little munchkins in. It wasn't long before they came back in to say that the little ones were way off in the woods. I shortened that phone conversation quite a bit and tore off through the woods.

When I found them, I scooped them up and headed back to the house, trying to keep from traumatizing the poor darlings in my panicked state of mind. We have this rule here that you can play in the woods as long as you can see the house.

Our property sits on the border of the National Forest deep in the mountains of Idaho, so it is possible for them to wander for quite a ways. That is why I panicked! Well, that and the fact that it's not exactly furry little Garfields that live in the mountains. Instead, these cats are not quite so friendly as that lovable fur ball.

But my one-year-old and three-year-old didn't understand that rule in its entirety and so had decided to go exploring. All in all, they really hadn't wandered very far. There were just so many trees I couldn't see them very well. Yet I was extremely happy to have them safe in my arms once again.

The older boys love to explore these woods, and I trust them to keep an eye on the distance between themselves and the house. It took a couple summers, though, to build up that trust. Quite a few times, I had to run after them to let them know they had gone a little too far. Considering that they were only three and five at the time, you can see why I didn't trust them too much.

One day I stepped outside to see where they were. I could hear voices from way off in the distance, but it wasn't in the direction of the woods behind our house. Instead, the voices were from across the road in the neighbor's woods. So I decided to follow the voices and see where my journey would take me.

I walked down the road to the spot where the creek flows underneath our road and over to the neighbor's property. The voices were coming from the creek bed on the *wrong* side of the road.

Now we also have another rule at our home here. It is the "Do not put a toenail on the road" rule. At least not until you're one of the "big" kids and have proven to be trustworthy. We live just a few yards off the road and that has a great potential for danger when it comes to four little kiddos. It has taken some consistent training around two years of age for every child to learn that the road is very, very dangerous, even deadly. One summer, it helped to drive home the point of how deadly the road can be when they saw one of their kittens get hit by a car. It was a very gross lesson but one that was well taken.

As I stood there listening to the voices from across the road, I wondered if the boys knew how much trouble they were going to be in for crossing the road. After yelling loud enough to get their attention, I soon began to see two little heads through the trees. They came walking up to me in the creek bed to where I stood on the road.

As I began to lay into them of how they had disobeyed and crossed the road, they showed me exactly how they had found a loophole in my rule. They calmly walked *under* the road through the culvert that the creek water runs through. I was astounded and also trying hard not to laugh! They had not disobeyed at all. They had simply been exploring and found what great fun it was to follow the dry creek bed to wherever it led them. And if the truth be told, I would have probably done the same thing as a child. It looked like so much fun! Even to me. And I'm supposed to be the mama.

So I took them back to Daddy and let him lecture them on how they could not go wandering all over the neighbor's property whenever they wanted. Ah, children. They will give you many moments of panic, of tears, and even more of laughter.

~~~~~~

Then there are the crazy things kids do that leave you baffled as to the point of it. Take for instance the remains of a sandwich I found in the toilet bowl the other day. Or how our littlest guy loved to chew on daddy's earplugs whenever he got the craving for rubber and ear wax. One son liked to blow bubbles in the toilet bowl. Several of them got into the bad habit of picking at their belly button.

When our second son was learning how to walk, he absolutely could not stay on his feet. It seemed he was always falling and tripping over his own toes. It was as though his brain were going faster than what his little legs could keep up with. One day, we decided to time how long he could stay on his feet. He made it to thirty seconds before he fell on his nose. He is now four years old and can run like the wind in spite of all his walking troubles.

He will leap from places nearly as high as he is and get back up and try it again. In the wrestling matches between him and his older brother, he may not always win, but he will put up the fight of the century trying. He will fight like a tiger on steroids even though his bigger brother is about thirty pounds heavier.

Children are such entertainment. On evenings when we are extremely bored and we've already played games all winter, read all the books we have within reach, and watched enough Don Knotts to last me a lifetime, we will sit and watch our children. But before you go make a habit of this, I will give you one warning. Your children will absolutely love it!

In fact, once they see that Dad and Mom are watching them, it will begin to escalate out of control. Each child will try to prove his or her toughness by doing some extreme feat. Every jump gets a little higher and every yell gets a little louder.

But it is such great fun! So the next time you are bored silly, go pop yourself a huge bowl of popcorn and sit down to some of the best stunts you have seen in a long time.

Cry when you must, smile when you can, and laugh when it's least expected!

"My little children, let us not love in word, neither in tongue; but in deed and in truth." (I John 3:18)

Sanity Tip: *Watch your children for the twenty-three hours and fifty-nine minutes that you can. Trust God for that one minute you missed because He has been watching all day anyway!*

Chapter 14

Truly Angels

This is a chapter I both dread and anticipate at the same time. It is a season of my life in which I first tasted the bitter-sweetness of death. Of losing a close loved one. Of losing a child.

God does not promise us an easy life. He did not say that we would never know heart-wrenching pain and nights filled with tears. But He did promise us Heaven. A chance to see our loved one again. That child who died in an accident. That baby who struggled for breath minutes after it was born. Or, like me, my babies whose first breath was that of the sweet scent of Heaven.

In this chapter, I am going to let you in on a part of my heart that I have not shared with many people. I wrote my thoughts in a journal during this time of my life, and I cannot read that journal or write this chapter without my heart breaking once again.

We found out I was pregnant a little more than eight months after we were married. I'll let my journal take it from there.

April 12, 2000

I had suspected that I was pregnant for about a week ... so on April 12, I took a pregnancy test. I was on my way to school to sub for Marc (my brother)—but I just couldn't wait another day to find out. So after Lowell left for work, I took the test. After two minutes, I could see the pink line! It was such a great feeling—I wanted to tell everyone. I left it lay in the bathroom all day. When Lowell got home, I called him to the bathroom. I said there was something I wanted him to see. We were so excited! God was sending us a precious package.

April 17, 2000

*I took a second pregnancy test—just to be sure. The blue line showed up even clearer! We were **really** pregnant!*

May 27, 2000

"... Only God knows just what they could have been."

We were so excited about a baby coming! I'd been to see the doctor a couple times ... I was having nausea throughout the day and feeling really tired all the time ... I had headaches more frequently—although not like a migraine. And sometimes I would get so short of breath—even from just talking. But it was such a wonderful feeling to be pregnant—there's nothing quite like it. You feel so alive! You are never lonely because you always carry a little one with you. We had planned and dreamed about the baby—who it would look like, how it would act. I had even bought a crib and swing at garage sales. But God knows best.

On May 14, Sunday, I woke up at 4:30 to find that I was bleeding. We called the doctor at 9:00. He said to take it easy. If I was still bleeding on Monday, I was to go in and see him. On Monday, I went to see the doctor. They did an ultra-

sound and couldn't see any heart activity. The doctor thought it was probably a threatened miscarriage. He sent me to the lab for blood so he could get my HCG level. Then on Thursday they would check it again. If it would rise—the baby was alive. If it would decrease—God had taken the baby home.

That was the beginning of a tough week. We had also found out the day before that Rose had delivered a baby boy but that he had died . (Rose was a good friend.) I tried to trust God with this little one—but I had wanted it so much, it was hard to let go.

Darl & Rose's baby's graveside service was at 4:30 p.m. I was to help sing in a quartet. We got there, and I was dreading it—just knowing we were probably going through the same thing. As we walked into the cemetery, we met Janet (she was there visiting). She said happily, "Congratulations, Kendra!" I said, "Uh-huh." Then I turned to Lowell and started crying. "I don't know if I can do this," I told him. He was so sweet—he put his arm around me and asked if I wanted to leave. But I wanted to be there for Rose and Darl. I made it through, although I didn't let myself dwell on the words of the songs because I would start choking up. I'm convinced that the Lord had an angel on both sides of me the whole time ... I have a feeling our baby and Darl's baby died on the same day. They lost their baby on Saturday. And as I look back now, that Saturday was the day I no longer felt pregnant ... I think God took our babies into His arms on the same day. I know He had a perfect reason for it—my girl is in a better land.

On Thursday I gave more blood so they could check my HCG level. All day I wondered if it was up or down. It was beginning to wear on me—the not knowing what was happening ... At 4:00 p.m. I called to find out about my HCG level. The nurse said my one from Monday was normal, but they hadn't gotten today's back yet. She would call on Friday with the report. What she said made me excited; I told Mom to cross her fingers.

But, alas, God had chosen Thursday, May 18, 2000, to let us know He held our little one in the palm of His mighty hand. At 4:30, I miscarried our baby ... I called Mom and Kris (my sister) ... it hit me finally. I had really lost my baby. They held me while I cried. I knew God now held her, but for the moment, I needed to grieve. I felt such a sense of loss. But it was more than that; I felt lonely. I missed having my baby with me all the time. It hurt so much—like having my heart torn open again. And yet there was relief—just knowing the uncertainty of it all was over.

Lowell came over and held me as we both cried. He was hurting to see me hurt, but I needed to grieve for my baby, or it would take a lot longer to heal from it. Some people think it shouldn't bother us much because it was so early—nine weeks along, but to me she was precious and sweet ... So tiny— so sweet—so vulnerable—so precious! I wanted to hold her forever. She was our little girl ... I always thought it would be a girl—I don't really know. But one day, the Lord put a name in my head: Amber. "Her name is Amber." Amber means "like a jewel; cherished." She seems to me a precious jewel that the Lord let us cherish for not only nine weeks, but the rest of our lives.

June 1, 2000

"... the Lord giveth and the Lord taketh away; blessed be the name of the Lord." It gave me peace to say this verse the last two weeks—just knowing God's in control, and He never makes a mistake. The last week has been good; I feel able to laugh, love, and live again. The future seems brighter as I hope and dream again. Yet I still have times when the sorrow over-takes me, and I allow myself to grieve once more for our dar-ling baby. I wonder what she looks like in heaven right now. What is she doing? Did she and Rose's Michael see Jesus' face at the same time? Does Jesus cradle her in His arms like I long to do someday? Oh, it makes me long for heaven—to see my little girl running toward me with a radiant smile on her face,

her curly hair bobbing up and down; and at last I reach her and wrap my arms around her tight as I hear her whisper in my ear, "Mama, I love you."

Several months passed before I wrote in the journal again. I was pregnant for the second time now.

November 17, 2000

I found out I was pregnant on October 7. We were so glad! But on Monday, October 23, we lost this second baby. We hadn't even told anyone yet ... Our parents had a grandchild and lost a grandchild all in one breath. I can't figure out why this has happened to us yet again. It doesn't seem fair. But I know one good thing that has come of it. I was holding too tightly to my dream of having children. I needed to give it up to God and His plan for our lives. I still struggle with it at times— but it's getting easier. I have to depend on His grace and strength to help me. Lowell has been wonderful to me. He hurts for me. The depression hasn't been as bad this time. I've tried to keep a smile on my face, but it's so hard. I miss my two sweet babies.

Sweet Babies

Sweet babies, you're gone—oh what shall I do?

Shall I mourn, shall I weep, shall I cry out for you?

My aching arms long to cuddle you close.

To count your fingers and kiss your pink nose.

Someday up in Heaven, my sweet ones, we'll meet.

And here's what we'll do at our dear Savior's feet.

We'll laugh and we'll giggle and hold hands all day.

Then I'll whisper the words I've been longing to say.

"My darlings, I love you."

~Your Mommy

November 25, 2000

"Dear Lord, it's me again. I'm still having trouble with letting it go. Lord, why did You take our two babies? It doesn't seem fair, Father, when other ladies can have babies whenever they want. Why us? Why did You pick us to bear this sorrow? It hurts too bad—not just the losing—but the reminders every day that I will not be having a baby on December 16 or June 16. December is coming up, Lord, and I don't know if I can bear the day that should have brought forth new life. Sometimes I want to get so angry and scream, "It's not fair!!" But that reminds me of a little child throwing a temper tantrum. Lord, even though it hurts, I want to be at peace. I want to be able to say, "Not my will, but Thine be done." And mean it. But I'll have to be honest with You. Right now, all I can do is say the words and mean it a little bit. Help me, Lord, to mean them someday with all my heart. I'll trust You, Lord, to work in my heart and change me."

January 6, 2001

"My substance was not hid from Thee, when I was made in secret, and curiously wrought in the lowest parts of the earth. Thine eyes did see my substance, yet being unperfect; and in Thy book all my members were written, which in continuance were fashioned, when as yet there was none of them." Psalm 139:15–16

I'm sitting in the dining area of Seven Springs Ski Resort in Pennsylvania. We've been planning this trip for a while with Kendalls. Lowell was really looking forward to it! But I can't ski. We just found out Thursday that I am pregnant again. I am excited but scared. Dr. Marlar said I should not go skiing—especially if we are afraid of another miscarriage. I feel better skipping skiing now than if we would lose the baby later. Oh, I hope we get to keep this one! Mostly because Lowell really wants a baby now. I want to dream about this child and get so excited—but I am so scared. It's as though I don't want to set myself up for another big crash. But in my head I need to trust the Lord.

May 20, 2001

I can't help crying as I read back over the pages in here. It's been just over a year since we lost our first baby. But when I read these pages written with tears, it all comes back again. Yet then I feel this baby move, and my heart takes hope. Hope that I will see this precious one within me someday!

That precious child was born several months later on September 18, 2001. God had answered our prayers.

I would go on to lose another baby in the next few years, but I also knew that while I held in my arms my children here on earth . . . He held in His arms my angels.

God promises a safe landing, not a calm passage.

"For as the heavens are higher than the earth, so are My ways higher than your ways, and My thoughts than your thoughts."

Isaiah 55:9

Sanity Tip: *If you have lost a little one, allow yourself to grieve. Bottled-up grief can swiftly turn into bitterness, and bitterness will eat your soul from the inside out. So don't feel guilty for days when you cry every hour. Just remember that, while you are reaching for that tissue, God has allowed these circumstances to shape you into a beautiful vessel that He can use.*

This poem was written out of the deep pain of loving and losing, yet after the pain, God brought healing.

The Scar

The wound—it was a sorry sight—so ugly, red, and bruised.

The blood spilled out and over as pain went coursing through.

In agony, I cried, "Oh, God, will this wound never heal?"

Until I saw the miracle His finger did reveal.

As over time His loving hand worked wonders in my heart.

And closed the wound—that gaping wound—which did so sting and smart.

But to bring healing to the wound He had to leave a scar.

And then I prayed, "Oh, Lord, it shall remind me who You are.

It'll teach me of the love it took for You to die for me.

It's a shadow of the scar You bore to set my lost soul free."

And as someday down the road of life, I turn my head to find

A wounded heart that's bleeding—then this scar shall come to

mind.

"Oh, God," I'll cry, "I then shall know Your reason for my

pain.

For from this scar shall come Your healing that will be my

brother's gain."

~ K. Graber

The Accident

The next few chapters do not have much to do with raising children. Instead, they are about a time in our lives when we walked through a dark valley. Indeed, we are still walking through it, but we can see the light at the end of the valley now. And for that we praise our Lord.

Chapter 15

Touched By God

The phone rang. I answered it and soon realized that this was "the call."

Now I've always wondered where I would be when "the call" came and how I would react. For those of you who have not spent nights wondering about such things, I shall try to bring you down to my level a bit.

"The call" has always been sometime in the future when I would find out that one of my children or my husband had been seriously injured or even killed. I'm hopeless, I know. But nights when I can't sleep and one thought leads to another, I'd picture how it would happen and what I would do. I could see myself collapsing to the floor in uncontrollable weeping or perhaps just simply passing out as the heroine does in novels.

The problem is—I am no heroine. And when I answered the phone to hear that Lowell had been in a motorcycle accident, I thought it was a joke. You see, I'm a blonde and tend to fall for jokes quite often. So I was trying to protect my pride somewhat and told Ken, Lowell's business partner, that he was pulling my leg. I simply thought Lowell had put him up to this as a great joke to play on me. After all, my husband has been known to pick on me—although I must confess that I pick right back.

Finally, Ken convinced me it was really true and that Lowell had indeed had an accident and was headed to the hospital with a broken elbow, ribs, and possibly pelvis. Now here is where I must tell you how I reacted. It wasn't anything like in my sleepless night visions. Instead I felt nothing. Absolutely nothing.

Now before you begin to think me a heartless wife, I will try to explain what I have since found out. Our minds can go into shock. It is as though they freeze with unexpected news such as this until we are able to process it rationally. So, yes, I froze. It was later that I felt myself begin to crumble. But we'll get to that.

I was also told that Lowell was conscious and talking and had been rather perturbed when the EMTs had cut off his new riding jacket. To tell you that I took joy in that precious fact in which my dear husband was ticked at someone may once again lead you to believe that I have no heart. But you must realize that I have been married to my best friend for almost ten years, and I can pretty much predict how he will react in certain circumstances.

And this was one of those circumstances in which he reacted exactly as I would have thought. So to hear that he was fuming because they cut his new jacket said to me that at least his brain was still intact. At that I breathed a sigh of relief because I knew right then that he at least did not have brain damage. That was one injury I could check off the list.

I hung up the phone and gathered the children around while I told them that Daddy had been in a motorcycle accident. We knelt on the floor, held hands, and prayed. As I raised my head from prayer, I saw a tear slip out of Derek's eye.

I quickly tried to get some clothes packed for the children as well as myself. It was a very scatterbrained packing party. In moments like that, when your brain is half-frozen, you need to just plan on forgetting something. After we packed, I dropped the children off at Jan's house, picked up Rebecca and Janet to go with me, met their husbands, and headed to the hospital in Canada. The accident had taken place along the Kootenay Bay in British Columbia, just north of our home in Idaho, so he was flown by helicopter to a hospital in Trail, British Columbia.

I tried to prepare myself before walking into the Emergency Room, but how does one do that exactly? I just remember that, as I stood talking to the receptionist, I began to feel hot, shaky, and lightheaded. My frozen brain was beginning to thaw.

A nurse took me and the wonderful friends who went with me back to the waiting room for families in the Emergency Room. Then they said I could go to him. In my mind's eye, I can still see him lying on that gurney. He was unconscious when I walked up to him on legs that were threatening to give way. Wires protruded at odd angles from his body, and an oxygen mask was on his face. The EMTs had tied a sheet around his pelvis since they were pretty certain he had broken it.

After a moment, he woke up and relief flooded his eyes as he saw me standing there. But that relief was soon replaced with a look of pain as he cried out, "It hurts!" We had had moments like this before when Lowell had broken bones and had been in pain but never this kind of pain. The pain was coming because of his internal bleeding, and that was scary. As I stood there putting cool washcloths on his forehead to help cool him down, he would pass in and out of consciousness. That was probably one of the hardest things I had to do, to stand there helplessly while waiting on the doctors to figure out if they were going to keep him there in Canada for surgery or ship him down to the USA. I did not feel right about them trying to ship him down to Spokane while he was still bleeding internally.

So I went back to speak with Ken and Rebecca, and Marcus and Janet about it. We all felt so very troubled since internal bleeding is not something you mess around with. Then Ken suggested that we pray. And with that prayer, God decided to work His first miracle.

It wasn't long before the doctor came in to say that they did not have room on the ICU floor and would need to transport him to Spokane that evening. Then he turned around and walked back out. Not a full minute later, the same doctor came back in to say that there had been a change, and they were doing surgery within an hour or two. It seemed that they could not get a doctor to accept him in Spokane, considering it was a Saturday evening. To us, it became very clear right then that whatever the doctor's motives might have been, God was still in control.

During surgery, they found everything intact. The internal bleeding had not been coming from a ruptured blood supply to his colon as they'd first thought. Instead, it was from the fractures in his pelvis, but the blood was contained and did not seem to be getting any worse. I breathed a sigh of relief that perhaps it wasn't as bad as I had begun to picture.

The next day, we finally heard a label put on his condition: *critical but stable.*

Whenever I had heard that in the past about someone else, I immediately assumed this person was on death's doorstep. And perhaps Lowell was and God mercifully kept me from knowing it. But I did not feel as though he was going to die.

He laid there with internal bleeding that was contained and we hoped stopped. He also had four ribs broken in several places each, a shattered elbow, multiple fractures in his pelvis, a punctured lung, four fractures in his right hand, and a chip of bone broken off in his ankle. He was on oxygen and had a chest tube to drain the fluid in his chest cavity. His left foot had no sensation whatsoever due to the sciatic nerve being pinched in his hip fractures. But God had decided to spare his life.

The second evening, I sent my wonderful friends to a motel to get some sleep since there wasn't much for them to do there at the hospital with me. I went to a small waiting room and lay down on the couch to try and sleep a couple hours.

As I lay there, my frozen state of mind began to thaw a little more. And as I thawed, I began to crumble. As I crumbled, I also began to weep. I wept for my husband lying in that ICU bed all broken up and hurting. I wept for myself and all the trauma I was going through and all the decisions I had to make. I wept because I was scared.

And then I felt Him.

I will never forget that feeling as long as I have breath in this body. A Presence so sweet, so poignant, and so comforting filled the room that it seemed as though I could reach out my hand and physically touch Him. In that tiny room, I felt the hand of my God reach down and touch the very essence of my soul.

And I knew I would never be the same.

Chapter 16

Leaning on those Arms

Monday morning, the hospital staff told us that they had found a doctor to accept Lowell at Sacred Heart Hospital in Spokane, Washington. I was overjoyed! We were going to an area I was more familiar with. We had a wonderful nurse that last day in Canada who tried her best to get us out of there and down to the USA. She knew we were more comfortable with the health care system there than in Canada.

I had the choice to either have Lowell transported by ambulance to Spokane, which would take three hours, or have him flown part way. As I was trying to make this decision, they decided that he needed more blood, so they gave him two more units. That made the decision for me. If there was any possibility of him bleeding internally again, I wanted him to get to Spokane as quickly as possible. So an ambulance was scheduled to drive him down to the border where the helicopter would pick him up and take him the rest of the way.

A couple hours before leaving, the helicopter radioed and said that, because of inclimate weather, they could not pick him up at the border. In fact, it was quite a ways from the border, which would mean more riding in the ambulance. I smile as I look back on it now. Remember the story where Jesus said, "Peace, be still?" Well, I want you to know that He still does that in the twenty-first century.

About twenty minutes later, the helicopter radioed back again to say that the weather had cleared enough that they could land at a town closer to the border. I was delighted … but God wasn't finished yet. Just as the critical-care team was wheeling Lowell down the hall to the ambulance, his kind nurse came over to me with tears in her eyes to hug me good-bye. She said that the helicopter had radioed that the clouds had lifted and that they could now land at the border! I felt a chill go through me as I realized exactly what our God had done. By the time we reached the border, the sun was shining beautiful-ly.

Once Lowell was in Spokane, they watched over him closely to make sure that his lungs were healed enough that they could proceed with surgery on his elbow and pelvis.

While waiting for surgery, a wonderful friend from church started a Carepage for Lowell. It was a website where I could post updates on his condition, and people could leave messages for us to read. I never knew such websites existed and was so very grateful for this one. We "met" people we hadn't heard from in years, and it was a fast, simple way to let people know how he was doing without being on my cell phone every ten minutes.

Throughout these few chapters, I am going to include some of those updates to give you a glimpse into this valley in which we found ourselves.

Update on May 14, 2008

For those of you who have not heard, I'll start at the beginning. Lowell was on a motorcycle road trip in Canada on Saturday with about 8 guys. Going around a switchback curve, he wiped out and headed off the other side. His bike hit a reflector sign, which launched him into the air where he flew 60– 70 feet off the road and 30 feet down a ravine toward the lake. The Lord must still have a purpose for him because he sailed between two trees and bounced on a smooth rock rather than one of the multiple jagged ones before landing on the ground. Those who were with him will testify that he had slowed down for the curve and had not been doing anything foolish. From multiple incidents through this whole thing, I firmly believe the Lord had a reason for letting Lowell wipe out on that road. I have never felt the Lord closer and more in control of a situation at any other time in my life. That may sound odd to say while my husband is lying in an ICU bed, but it is true nonethe-

less. I have a God who's so much bigger than all these decisions I have to face.

Lowell was life-lined to Trail, BC, Canada. He was taken into surgery that night for internal bleeding in his abdomen. They thought he might have ruptured the blood vessel to his colon, but when they opened him up, they found it to be perfect, and the bleeding was from his fractured pelvis. He has 4 ribs broken in a couple places each, a shattered elbow, a pelvis broken in 4 places, including his hip socket, a dislocated ankle, and a chip broken off his lower backbone. He has a pulmonary contusion, which I believe is bruising of the lungs, resulting in hematomas in his chest. He has a chest tube in to drain that and is on oxygen, plus a bunch of other wires and gadgets. He has a bit of fluid in his lungs that they believe is a direct result of the trauma to his lungs. They are waiting until his lungs are stronger before scheduling surgery for his hip, elbow, and possibly pelvis.

You all may pray that the Lord would heal him quickly, that he would not get pneumonia, and that he can have good spirits through it all. He is going to be in this hospital for probably a week and possibly in a rehab. facility after that. Please pray that the Lord would help me as I make decisions, both medical and financial. I've never been in a situation like this before, but the Lord has shown His hand mighty through this time. Also pray for the children as they are away from both of us. I will be able to go home a bit more now that Lowell is not in such critical condition.

To the best of our ability, we have tried living our lives in the center of God's will. God brought us together 9 years ago, gave us 4 beautiful children, moved us 2,000 miles from our family, and now has Lowell lying in this hospital bed for some reason beyond our human comprehension. I cannot express to you how strongly I feel this is just another stepping stone that God has put in our life's pathway.

I want to thank all of you who have been praying and who have offered to help. We have a wonderful church that has been here for us. God put them in our lives for such a time as this! And we have felt the prayers of our family back east and also appreciate the many offers of help from you. We cannot help feeling so extremely small with the generosity of all our family, friends, and church family.

It was now Wednesday evening, and I was going to see my precious children for the first time since Saturday. I missed them but also knew that they were being well cared for. Besides, I also knew that they were not missing me nearly as much as I was missing them! In all reality, just knowing that they were not pining away for Dad and Mom left me better able to concentrate on Lowell and the decisions I needed to make about him.

Another wonderful friend from church had driven two and a half hours that morning to come down to Spokane and take me out for lunch. It felt so very good to talk with her and share some burdens on my heart. Afterward, she asked if I needed anything at Wal-Mart. So I grabbed the chance to buy a couple small toys for the children.

I knew they were not at all excited about coming to see Daddy at the doctor. Back then, they were not used to hospitals, and I'm sure Sacred Heart seemed big, smelly, and scary to them. So I bribed them to come see us by telling them I'd have a surprise for them. You can fault me for that if you wish, but I was desperate to get a glimpse of my four sweet children. And, as you know, desperate people can go to desperate measures to get what they want! Besides, I was suffering a deficiency in slobbery kisses.

That evening Lowell's mother and sister came to visit us. His mom was able to stay only a couple days, but his sister was able to stay for two weeks. When our wonderful babysitters brought our children to see us, Lowell's sister went home with them and the children. She stayed home with them until Lowell was discharged from the hospital.

Being able to see Lowell's mother was exactly what I needed at that time. Mothers can do something for their children that even wives can't even if the child is thirty-one years old.

I was also feeling weary from answering requests for decisions from doctors, nurses, social workers, and financial advisors. In our marriage, Lowell has been the one to make the final decisions on major events in our lives, but now he was lying in an ICU bed, and I was required to make these on my own. Don't get me wrong; I had great advice and support from Ken, Lowell's business partner, as well as our church family.

But I was used to discussing things with Lowell, and in his current condition, he was not able to make decisions. Not only could he not think clearly because of all his medications and the trauma to his body, but also, the medical staff, as well as our deacon, thought it wise not to tell him the full extent of our financial situation.

That was one of the hardest things I've had to do—keep something from him what he wanted to know. When he was better able to handle it, I did tell him what we had found out after numerous phone calls to our insurance companies. We are a part of a Christian sharing group called Samaritan Ministries. They are wonderful, Godly people who helped us tremendously. Through an oversight on our part, this accident was not able to be covered. However, they told us to send it in, and they would put it on the monthly statement as a special prayer need. It was so kind of them and gave me the faith that God would somehow help us pay for the rest.

In a hospital, you never know when or where you might have the chance to witness. One day I was called out of Lowell's ICU room to speak with the social worker. She was a kind lady, but I could tell she was really beginning to feel sorry for us poor people without insurance coverage. She was trying to come up with multiple ways that this might be covered when I quietly told her that our God is much bigger than hospital bills. I will never forget that kind woman's reaction. Perhaps she was a Christian, perhaps not. Either way, I wanted her to know Who I was depending on. I knew that if I could see this mountain from God's perspective, it would look very different indeed.

Update on May 15, 2008

The orthopedic surgeon was in and said that they can get Lowell into surgery tomorrow afternoon. Finally! It seems as if we are waiting for that to happen so he can be on the final road to recovery.

We are praising our precious Lord for holding us in His hand during this difficult time but mostly for keeping our wonderful husband and daddy alive!

Update on the morning of May 16, 2008

It's Friday morning, and Lowell is awaiting surgery. The doctor came in and said that it is scheduled for 1:00 p.m. So we would appreciate your prayers once again as he goes into major surgery for his left elbow and left hip socket.

The ortho doctor was in last evening and talked with us for quite a long time. He showed Laura, Lowell's mom, and I the 3-D x-rays of his pelvis. It was extremely interesting! There is a piece of bone broken off of his sacrum, which is his lower spine. It is just simply floating in there and has caused the sciatic nerve to be pinched or pulled.

And then his left hip socket is broken and pulled apart. They will need to screw that back together. There are several pieces they will need to fit together like a puzzle.

His left elbow is (in the doctor's words) "cornflakes." It is going to require a plate and screws. There is nothing they can do for his ribs except to hold still—which is going to get harder and harder for my athletic husband. His left ankle may

187

have a fracture in it although they weren't sure from the x-rays yet. They plan on doing more x rays on the ankle while in surgery.

He was complaining of his right hand hurting, so they x-rayed it yesterday. The report came back that there is a fracture in the bone to his littlest finger. There may be two other possible fractures in his hand. He is still using his hand, so these fractures are not really bad. The doctor said that he may keep finding fractures, especially when he gets up and begins rehab.

As far as his attitude, we cannot be more thankful. He has been in excellent spirits! Reading all the messages and emails people have sent is very encouraging to all of us. He just threw a used tissue at me, so he is definitely on the road to recovery, although he is still in quite a bit of pain. He said that his pain-med. button is his best friend.

I'm typing for Lowell as he's talking to me here: "I'm humbled and very thankful for the way people have reached out to us. If I wasn't on heavy-duty painkillers, I'd say more."

He definitely hasn't lost his sense of humor!

Lowell's mom and I waited and waited for surgery to be done. It was a special time for us. We were able to sit down in the cafeteria and catch up on our lives a bit. The surgery took longer than expected, and I have never seen a more fatigued doctor than the one who walked toward me that evening to give me the report.

Update on the evening of May 16, 2008

It is 9:00 p.m. on Friday night, and I am rather tired as I type this. So when I reread it in the morning, I'll probably be embarrassed at how befuddled it sounds! Oh well, that's a woman for you. We've had a long afternoon and evening waiting for surgery to begin and waiting for it to end.

We can give all the credit to our Lord for a successful surgery! Lowell got out of surgery and into the recovery room about 45 minutes ago. He will be brought up to his ICU room at least for the night and will probably be moved to the ortho floor tomorrow.

The surgeon said the surgery went very well. Before going into surgery, he told us that (from the x-rays) Lowell's shattered elbow was the worst he had seen. After surgery, he said it was a disaster, but they got it looking like an elbow again by putting in a plate (or plates) and lots of screws. His left hip socket was screwed together. The sciatic nerve had been pinched in his broken socket, so we hope that the sciatic pain will be much better from now on. That was Lowell's main complaint today.

They put a screw or two in his left ankle. And this morning they x-rayed his right hand and found a couple fractures in it, so during surgery, they put a cast on it. He doesn't know that yet, and quite frankly, I'm not sure I want to be here when he finds out! Perhaps I'll play hooky ... he had been so very glad that he could at least use his right hand to do a few things, such as (in his own words) "pick his nose"!! Now he'll probably want me to do that. I'll try to be the Proverbs 31 woman and do it for him, I guess. This accident hasn't taken much of the orneriness out of him, as his visitors can testify.

Update on May 17, 2008

We have finally moved out of ICU!! I never knew changing hospital rooms could be such an exciting event. The children were here while he was getting transferred and stressed him out pretty bad. Jeff and Yolanda came and took the children to Coeur d'Alene where Ken and [wife] were going to meet them. They also went out and bought Lowell a fan since his room is so hot. I think they were angels in disguise today!

After they moved him, he had a fever of 101, so he was miserable right then, but it is now back down to 99.2. We're still working at making sure he doesn't catch pneumonia.

Lowell's pain is probably the worst that it's been today. They are taking him off of morphine and onto another painkiller that probably isn't quite as strong. So if you wish for specific prayer requests, his pain would be one of them. He has a high pain tolerance, but I think his ouies now take the cake.

You could also pray that the Lord would keep our children and me healthy as we are apart. We appreciate all the prayers, gifts, and offers of help—especially with our four children. We couldn't ask for better friends and family. Everyone has been so encouraging, and we can feel you holding us up in prayer.

Update on May 18, 2008

It's a beautiful, positively gorgeous day outside here in the good, ol' northwest! Lowell slept well last night.

Lowell's wonderful nurse couldn't believe they had cut his PCA (his pain button of a type of morphine) so quickly. He was in a huge amount of pain yesterday afternoon. So for those of you who visited him yesterday, you probably saw him at his very worst. He was in much better spirits last night and woke up this morning saying he will be home by next weekend. I just said, "Uh-huh, we'll see." I've found out you don't want to argue with a man on morphine! One thing is for sure; when he makes up his mind about something, there is no stopping him. So, Lord willing, home we will go.

I must tell you, though, that Lowell really likes the nurse who was sitting beside him during the night. She's sort of blonde, blue-eyed, 5'4", and weighs ... well, never mind. You get the picture. I'm wondering if I couldn't just take a test right now and get some kind of license to make me a "real" nurse. I have gotten the opportunity to learn so many things about the human body and all the drugs they put in it. I've also been able to do a few things that would perhaps qualify me as ¼ of a nurse. One thing I don't think I could do though, is be a nurse or doctor and not believe in a Creator. How the human body repairs itself is beyond amazing! We have been so intricately and tenderly formed by a wise and loving God. It is an absolute fool who can look at a newborn babe or a smashed body that's healed and working again, and say there is no God. To say it happens by chance takes more faith than it does to say that it was lovingly fashioned by an all-knowing Creator.

Lowell and I were talking again last night about how we cannot shake this feeling that there is a higher reason behind this accident. The Lord told us that His ways are higher than our ways, and this is one of those ways that we don't understand now, but we believe we will someday. Lowell feels deeply that if his pain can help bring one soul to the Lord, it is worth it. When you or one of your loved ones comes within inches of death, you realize how terribly short life truly is.

I also feel so very humbled with how everybody has encouraged us. When it seems we appear to be strong, it is not because WE are strong. It is simply because of our Lord and because of YOU. There are so many incredible people standing behind us, holding us up, both in prayer and in simply being there. I turn into a puddle of tears just thinking of our church family who has done so much more than their fair share in all of this. And also of our family back east who has either come out to help or are praying for us. We could not have done it without you! Thanks.

Update on May 19, 2008

Lowell got out of bed this morning and had his first wheelchair ride. It took a while to get his equilibrium back since he's been flat on his back for more than a week now. I pushed him out in the hospital hallway for a few minutes. At first he was pretty dizzy and nauseated, but that settled down after a while.

So he's back in bed now and trying to sleep a bit before lunch. A physical therapists will be in to work with him again around 3:00. I don't think he's looking forward to that very much. The ortho doctor said he can't have any weight on his left hip, left arm, and right wrist, and to just toe-touch on his left foot. That means the only extremities he can put any weight on are his right leg and right elbow. I can already see that the next 3 months are going to be very interesting!

Update on May 20, 2008

The Lord has brought us through another night and into a brand-new day! Lowell is sitting in his wheelchair waiting for the physical therapists to put him back in bed. I pushed him around in the hallway again. He has been up longer than he was yesterday and he is tolerating it much better. He is off of his oxygen, and they are still talking of sending him home near the end of this week.

We got him cleaned up this morning, brushed his teeth, and tried to shave him. I have never fully shaved him before.

When he was in ICU, I tried trimming his beard, and he finished the rest. But since his right hand is splinted because of the fractures, I got to be his barber today. I got all of my equipment ready—razor, shaving cream, hot towel, and a bowl of warm water. Just as I was ready to begin, I swung my arm around and knocked over the bowl of water! It went all down the front of my dress and sweater and made a big puddle on the floor. Once I'd settled down, I successfully shaved him, although I was afraid I'd cut him. But he is happy with his freshly shaved chin, and that's all that matters.

It seems we have gone through a myriad of emotions this past week and a half. We are so thankful that Lowell is alive and will mostly recover. When we think of all that could have gone wrong, it strengthens our faith that God has a purpose for this pain. We've also wondered, why us? And why did it have to be on a motorcycle? Although the guys with him will testify that he wasn't doing anything crazy, it's still people's first thought when they hear "motorcycle accident." It would have seemed much more "holy" to have gotten hurt while fixing a neighbor's roof, for instance. Yet I cannot say that I would wish it had not happened, for we have grown so much closer to our Lord, and He has been working in our hearts. You know, we all tell ourselves that we are not prideful, but then something like this happens to prove that, indeed, the "pride of life" was lurking deep within us. I do not wish to go back to the way it was before, because, although it hurts while God is working in our hearts, we know it is to make us more like Him.

Another reason I do not wish this had never happened is because of all the people we have been able to witness to. Lowell has stood on the brink of eternity and has come back with a new boldness to let others know of our precious Lord who gave him another chance to serve Him. When you or a loved one comes so close to going Home, you realize what is really important in this life: talking to a stranger, helping a neighbor, hugging your little girl, or taking your boys fishing. Life is not about how much money we can make, how success-

ful we are, or how much people admire us. It is simply trying to make the Father smile in everything we do—helping another soul to Heaven.

May God bless all of you who take this time to read my rambling thoughts, because that's what these updates truly are—I type as I think. Crazy, I know!

Update on May 21, 2008

Lowell slept very well last night and is already working on moving his legs as a form of his own physical therapy. Pillows have been invaluable for propping up his broken parts. In fact, at any given time, he has between 6 and 8 in his bed.

Breakfast is coming within the hour—scrambled eggs, bacon, toasted English muffin with jam, coffee, and a fresh-fruit cup. I have been his "feeding nurse" so far, although I think I'm about to get fired. After 10 days in the hospital, I'm only now beginning to get it right. The straw needs to be at just the right angle or he gets coffee, juice, and water splattered all over his face and chest. Then last night I dropped mashed pota-

toes on his leg as I was waving the spoon from tray to mouth. I

wouldn't blame him if he fired me, although I can't say I'd miss

the paycheck—come to think of it, he hasn't paid me yet.

We have been snacking on Jan's homemade banana

bread. Delicious! And she even put in chocolate chips—that

must have been for my benefit. Those of you who know me also

know that chocolate is usually a fixture at our house. A couple

days into this here "event," Lowell was telling me what an an-

gel I've been. I just told him that I expect to get a lot of choco-

late from all of this.

Update on May 22, 2008

Tomorrow is the day!!! Lord willing, they are going to

get us out of here tomorrow—Friday. This has been quite an

experience here in the hospital. I'm sure we'll never forget it.

But I know we are far from over. Lowell will be wheelchair-

bound for 3 months. So for you hunters who are already count-

ing forward 3 months, yes, he will be walking by opening day. He'll be starting to walk, but I doubt he will be hiking at all. But the doctor did say he would probably be able to pull a bow back within the next 4 months! I think that really made his day.

Yesterday, the physical therapist was here and worked his left leg and hip too much. A few hours later, his leg, hip, and pelvis were tight, and he was having spasms. "Yours truly" massaged it a bit and the nurse brought ice to put on it. He had a couple extra pain pills and slept really well through the night. I was able to go to the motel for the night. The motel is located close to the hospital, which makes it very convenient for me. Some families from church reserved 10 or so days there for us. Just that gesture makes us feel so overwhelmed with gratitude. I don't even know who all paid for it, but I do know they are some of the best Christians you'll ever meet.

As I was saying earlier, we are far from over in this "growing experience." He will need help getting in and out of his wheelchair, chair, bed, or wherever he decides to land. Oc-

cupational therapy has a little band they can attach to his right hand splint that holds a spoon, so perhaps he will at least be able to feed himself. I plan on making him a lot of smoothies and shakes that he can drink with a straw, just to make it a bit easier for him. I do know that I will be able to skip any exercise routine I had planned for summer since just lifting him and setting him down will be exercise enough. For those of you who are sitting there wondering how I, a short little gal, can lift my 175-pound husband, I want you to know I don't really lift him. We're getting our technique down where we link right arms, and I pull him up to a standing position, and then he pivots on his one good leg around to his wheelchair/chair and I help lower him. We did it for the first time alone yesterday, and it was a tad bit scary—it sure is a lot different than lifting Logan, our 18-month-old. But we'll get it down to an art, and Lowell will keep getting stronger every day.

We are going to have an interesting 3 months ahead. But I am one of those who doesn't think about something until it's staring me in the face. One day at a time is all I can handle. I'll leave tomorrow up to God. And for those days where I will be feeling overwhelmed, I'll just call up one of my good friends at church and whine a bit! So you ladies can consider yourselves forewarned.

Gotta run! Lowell's breakfast just arrived, and my coffee drink is almost gone.

Update on May 23, 2008

Lord willing, this is the last update you will read from the hospital. We are planning on leaving here to head home sometime this late forenoon or early afternoon. God has been so very good to us through all of this!

We will continue to keep this page updated for a bit once we get home, although my time will be taken up with quite a few other things. We'd like to thank everyone who helped us in so many big and little ways. Ladies who brought food into the hospital for me, those who paid for our motel, the ones who watched our children, ladies who brought casseroles in to Krissa at home, the young man who mowed our yard, the people who kept our vehicles filled with gas, those who built wheelchair ramps for our house and provided the handicap equipment, those who supported us in Canada, and especially those of you who called and prayed. I'm sure I missed somebody or something, but we want you to know how grateful we are to everyone's support. May God continue to bless you for blessing others.

Chapter 17

Even when He was Silent

Lowell was in the hospital for a total of 13 days. He went home with stainless steel screws and plates in his left elbow, hip, and ankle, as well as a removable cast on his right hand. He could not put weight through his left hip for three months and so was confined to a wheelchair and then crutches. As I mentioned earlier, Lowell's sister watched the children for the last week he was in the hospital. Once we got home, my mother was there to help us. These two were angels in disguise! My mother was able to stay for three weeks, and I'm not sure what I would have done without her.

We had many new and different things to adjust to. I was now Lowell's sole caregiver. I was in charge of his bathing, bathroom time, dressing, and medications. I had not prepared myself for how emotionally and physically exhausting it can be to take care of your spouse. It is so much different than taking care of a newborn, that's for sure.

I remember the first time I tried helping Lowell get out of the recliner and into the wheelchair all by myself. I stand only 5' 3½" (you *must* add the ½"), and he is 5' 9". Besides that, he's a good fifty pounds heavier than I, so you can see why I got a little apprehensive just trying to move him. I had visions of him falling and breaking something again. We tease each other about it now that, should he fall and I'm around, I will try to provide a soft landing for him.

Update on May 24, 2008

Hey, we actually made it home!! I can't remember when home looked so good. Just seeing all our sweet children again, my own bed, and, hey, even my very own shampoo. I'm picky, I know. But it's those little things that make up life as we know it and give us the comforts of home. Right now, Lowell is reclining within the comfort of our Lazy Boy. That's where he landed when we threw him in the door yesterday. Nah, just kidding! We very carefully lowered each body part until they were all resting peacefully in the cushiness of the recliner. That sounds a little better, doesn't it?

The ride home went well, with Lowell sleeping most of the way. We stopped once to readjust some pillows, and I accidentally bumped his broken ribs. That was a no-no! Problem is, he has so many parts that I need to avoid. Perhaps it would be easier if I spray-painted each part a bright pink.

Last night he slept in the recliner. The night went well. I didn't even have to get up to give him his meds every three hours; he did it himself. That was great, especially since I had Megan flopping around in bed with me.

Lowell would like to go to church tomorrow, but we take things a day at a time—sometimes an hour at a time. It would be wonderful to go to church, but I also don't want to wear him out.

It was one of those times when I had a little munchkin in bed with me, and I was so exhausted that I did not wake up when Lowell needed me in the middle of the night. I would put his meds in little Tupperware bowls beside his recliner so that he could take them every three hours himself without me having to wake up.

This time he needed me to help him use the restroom. After yelling for quite some time, he finally resorted to throwing his Tupperware bowls at my bedroom door in hopes that I would eventually wake up. It still didn't work—I was out cold. He somehow managed the restroom time on his own. And he had quite the pitiful story for me when I came out of my room the next morning to find Tupperware bowls scattered all over the hall. I did feel bad that he couldn't get me when he needed me, and yet I wanted to laugh at the same time. It felt good to laugh every once in a while.

It also wasn't long before I began to feel my brain starting to fry. I mentioned how physically and emotionally exhausting it was. Nobody warned me of how my brain would start to short circuit after trying to remember to give Lowell five different medications on five different timetables. And then there were the "fun" things to remember such as laxatives and stool softeners. I didn't want to skip a day or double the dose another day because the poor guy was in agony as it was without me screwing up all his pills.

Update on May 29, 2008

I finally have a few precious minutes to myself and thought I'd quickly post another update. It's amazing how God makes us humans able to adapt to our circumstances. Daily life is coming around to a new "normal," although there are a few things carried over from "life before," such as me needing my coffee to keep me awake during the day. When these 3 months

are up, I'll probably need to go through some kind of Coffee
Anonymous program.

The children are just as active and ornery as they al-
ways have been, except that now it's mostly up to me to do the
training. I'm thinking of putting myself on vacation once Low-
ell can begin to walk again. This has given me a respect for
those who must raise their children without a spouse. I'll either
be as tough as nails or completely bald!

Although the children are still running around like a
band of Indians, there is one person that I know won't get far.
Lowell usually is up about once a day to use the restroom and
then lands back in his recliner until the next restroom break.
We are thinking of trying to put him in the shower later today
since he says he's beginning to smell like an outhouse. I can't
blame him for wanting one since he hasn't had a good, real
shower in almost 3 weeks.

He was adventurous on Sunday and wanted to try go-
ing to church for the preaching service, so we began the spit

bath and dressing routine around 8:00 a.m. By the time we were done with that, plus his breakfast and shave, it was about 10:00 a.m. We think like turtles—slow and easy gets you there.

It was wonderful to be able to go to church, and everyone made us feel like we'd finally come back home. We don't know what we'd do without our church family. God put them and others in our lives for such a time as this!

Update on June 2, 2008

We called the doctor this morning to see if we could get an appointment today. Lowell's left leg is beginning to wake up out of its 3-week sleep and is nearly driving him crazy, short trip though it may be. (Those of you who didn't get that comment ... don't ask.) Anyway, they got us an appointment at 1:45 p.m, so we left all the kiddos with Mom and flew down there. That is, we hovered just slightly over the speed limit.

We also visited Costco for diapers and baby wipes. Then we proceeded to get lost trying to find the doctor's office.

Not really lost—we just went the wrong way. I have become such a country hillbilly that driving in a big city such as Spokane is pushing the limit of my sanity. Lowell wasn't much help, considering that he'd taken some pain pills and his leg felt on fire. The guy has felt pretty miserable the last 3–4 days. He has been sick to his stomach from his pain meds, and the sciatic nerve is coming back in his left leg. He said it feels like a hot poker down his leg. But it is good pain since he now has feeling in 3 of his 5 toes. I told him to think of it like a woman does in labor—the pain is good, right? To put it mildly, he did not appreciate that comment.

We got to see the x-rays for the first time since his surgery. Suffice it to say, it was gross. The x-ray of his elbow was disgustingly fascinating. When they told us they put screws in it, I was thinking the kind of screws that hold glasses together, like the ¼-inch kind. Excuse me, but this looked like nails! Lowell will probably read this post tomorrow and say that I exaggerated a bit, but that is the thought that came to mind when I first saw it. We'd really like to get the x-rays on a disk so we can look at them again at home! Makes for great enter-tainment on long winter nights.

The physician's assistant gave us a prescription for some generic Neurontin—a pain med specifically for nerve pain. So, Lord willing, he will begin to get a little relief from his sciatic pain—especially since she said it could last 2 months.

Lowell felt smugly happy when the x-ray of his right hand looked really good with new bone growing around a frac-ture. I say "smugly" because I had been reminding him not to put weight on it and also to wear his splint (which had been off more than on lately). Just trying to do my job as a nurse ... guess I'd better do my job as a wife now and be quiet about some things. He really does know what he's doing as far as how much he can do with broken bones, considering that he's had enough in his lifetime to pretty much write a manual on it. But everything looked good, and now he has some new pain

meds and (without doc's orders) some crutches. He even hob-
bled into the house on them—then nearly passed out on his
chair. Well, not quite. He was a little lightheaded—it just
makes a better story to say that he nearly passed out!

Okay, I think I need to go to bed since this is beginning
to not make much sense. Good night, all!

Update on June 6, 2008

It looks as if we are now on our own for a bit. Mom left
this morning to fly back home to Dad in Indiana. We appreci-
ated her being here so very much! She was here while I gave
Lowell his first spit bath, his first shower, his first church ser-
vice, and for the doctor appointments when we just picked up
and left within the hour. It was incredibly wonderful just to
have her here to watch the kids while I did things for Lowell. I
feel a little more confident that we can handle most of it now
that it's become a routine for us. But I also know that I can call

on a church full of people, as well as multiple neighbors, who would love to come help us.

Here's how our day begins. I usually have one of the three older children sleep on Daddy's side of the bed with me. They take turns every night, and I'm in big trouble if I forget whose turn it is! At 6:00 a.m. (give or take a half hour), another little person pitter-patters downstairs to snuggle in bed with Mom, just in time for Logan to wake up in his crib. Once the body count reaches four in my bed, I'm out of there. Little kids are none too gentle on the ribs!

Coffee comes next. And if I'm really good, I might even get dressed and my hair combed before Lowell needs his pain meds and breakfast. Then all the kiddos need breakfast, and our day truly begins. Lowell usually gets up several times a day to use the restroom and maybe sit in the office a bit. But for the better part of 24 hours, he is in his recliner.

We went to see our family doctor yesterday because Lowell was complaining of a sore throat. The doctor said it looked like a fungus that came about because of antibiotics he had been on. So we are to keep an eye on it, and he will prescribe a Nystatin gargle/flush if it gets worse.

Lowell has also been feeling a sharp pain in his left shoulder blade. We asked the doctor if the nerve that runs through his left elbow, where they did major surgery, would originate back there. He said that 3 nerves run through the arm and hand and they are all joined right back there in the shoulder blade. So, we hope it means he may be able to extend the fingers on his left hand since it seems to be nerves that are keeping him from doing that at the moment.

The most mentally exhausting component of the whole accident was Lowell's pain. I tried to speak of it in a lighthearted way in our updates, but, in all reality, it was very, very hard. His sciatic nerve had been pinched in his hip fracture for almost a full week until the doctor could do surgery, so he had some major healing to do.

About two weeks after we got home from the hospital, his leg began to wake up. The nerve was beginning to heal, but with that came some of the most severe pain he has ever been in. He described it as when you've sat on your leg too long, and it falls asleep. Then when you get up, it begins to "wake up" with that pins-and-needles-and-burning sensation. Now multiply that by a thousand.

The problem is that with nerve pain, there are not many medications that will help it. You simply have to wait, and wait, and wait. I saw my once very active, fit husband turn white, shaky, and sweating with the severity of his pain. And there was *nothing* I could do about it.

That was when I reached the end of my rope. I kept telling myself I would not cry in front of him. It would only cause him more distress. But as I was helping him in the bathroom one day, the tears began to fall and there was no stopping them. I looked at my husband, who stood there white as a sheet and ready to collapse at any moment, and I sobbed. I felt as though my guts were being ripped out and I could not go on. The dam had broken, and there was no holding it back.

Lowell just looked at me through sunken eyes as I cried out, "This isn't fair!" I wanted to stomp my foot, shake my fist, and yell that we had not asked for this. This simply wasn't how I had planned my life.

I cried out to God, but it seemed as though the heavens were shut. He was so silent, so very silent.

During those couple months when it seemed that I lived only from hour to hour, trying to help relieve Lowell's pain just a bit, I learned about the prayers the Spirit offers on our behalf. "But the Spirit itself maketh intercession for us with groanings which cannot be uttered" (Romans 8:26b), Sometimes all I could do was whisper the name of Jesus out of the agony of my heart. Other times I had no words, only tears. Yet I knew God heard my spirit crying out for Him.

And through it all, God was still God. He did not answer when I wanted Him to, yet I knew He was there. I *believed* He was there. And in His own time, He answered.

Update on June 11, 2008

I really wanted to get this update posted yesterday, which was the 1-month anniversary of the accident. It's hard to believe it's been a month already, yet at the same time, it feels a lot longer.

Lowell is still having some severe sciatic pain down his left leg. He called the ortho's office yesterday and talked to a nurse. She talked with the doctor who is convinced that the nerve med, "Neurontin" will work. The physician's assistant, the ortho doctor himself, and our family doctor all said it takes around 2 weeks to notice if it's working. Lowell has only been on Neurontin, a little more than a week now, so we are still holding out hope that he will feel better within the next week. As for his other broken sites, he hardly notices them at all. Ei-

ther they are not hurting anymore or the sciatic pain overrides those other pains.

And it also seems that we are continuing our reputation from this past winter by catching another flu bug! Logan threw up once on Saturday and then was fine, playing and being as ornery as ever. So since Lowell felt good enough to go to church Sunday, we went. Then yesterday, Terrel threw up—just one time and then he was fine. So at least this isn't a really long-lasting stomach flu. Problem is, you never know exactly where to set the bucket or lay the towel because you don't really know who is going to be looking at their lunch leftovers next.

We are expecting my sister, Krista, and her family on Saturday, so we are praying that all is well here before they arrive! I will try to post another update while they are here, but I can't promise it. Just don't go thinking we've all flown over a cliff if you don't hear anything for a week or more!

P.S. I almost forgot to mention that we had snow here yesterday—in JUNE!!! If you don't believe me, look at the pic-

tures I posted. That is the view I have right outside my kitchen window. A little slushy snow came down around the house, but it didn't stick. Snow in June can depress me if I let it, or I can believe that, once again, God has a purpose for it. I wonder if He isn't having a bit of fun with this idea of global warming this year!

Update on June 13, 2008

We woke up to some gloriously brilliant sunshine! It was shining in beautifully at 6:30, although the sky begins to lighten up before 4:00 a.m. right now. If you're wanting sleep, don't come to Bonners Ferry in the summer. Daylight is from 4:00 a.m. to 10:00 p.m. When we first moved here, I would be up with the baby around 3 or 4 a.m. The first night, I just thought we had a really bright full moon. After a week of "full moons," I realized it was actually the sun coming up! All you Idaho natives can laugh at me, that's okay.

As I was sitting in the living room this morning trying to adjust to the bright sunshine after a week of rain, Terrel came up to me. Now for those of you who don't know Terrel, he is our almost-five-year-old. He is the one who has a will of iron with a heart of sugar! This morning he looked at me with a face full of trusting innocence and said, "Mom, God knows a way to make everything just right!" Ahh, you should've seen the puddle my heart made on the floor. Sometimes children see things that we as adults have too much "knowledge" to comprehend. From the mouths of babes....

Summer is made for popsicles and sprinklers, right? At least, that's what the little Grabers here think. Today has been full of radiant sunshine, and the kiddos have already been out with the hose and wading pool ... although I did see some water get sprayed on my clean windows. They had been asking for popsicles ever since we got home from town this morning, but I told them they had to have some cheese first. I am still trying to get a bit of good nutrition in them in spite of our mixed-up lives right now. One cannot live on Cheetos and popsicles alone, right? But I figured they couldn't be too hungry since they had had a little snack not too long before. I told Derek they probably weren't even hungry yet, anyway. To which he said, "No, we're not really hungry yet. We'd just like something cold, like popsicles!" Uh-huh, Mom could see through that one.

For those of you who were praying for us last evening, I'd like to say thanks. Lowell's pain was so severe we had to call our family doctor again. We also talked with a couple people who gave us some ideas to try for his sciatic pain. It seems as if the nerves in his left leg and foot are waking up. That is good but so very painful. The pain runs down his left leg into his foot and toes, with the most severe pain being below his knee. He says the pain is always there just under the surface, but the times when it gets severe, it feels like electricity shooting down his leg, foot, and through his toes. We are expecting a call back from the nurse at the ortho doctor's office today. She may have some ideas to help or a new med to try. It looks as if his Neurontin may not be helping at all. So we would appreci-ate prayer in that regard. By the time this pain subsides, one of us will probably have gone nuts! Let's just hope it's not both of us.

Lowell and I were reading the first chapter of Job the other evening when we got to the last verse. "In all this Job sinned not, nor charged God foolishly" (Job 1:22). Our cir-cumstances right now are nothing compared to what Job was going through in his day. Yet he sinned not. That is the intent of our hearts—that we would not bring dishonor to the name of Jesus, but that all praise and glory should go to the One who has shown Himself both to us and to those watching these events. There is no other way to describe how we have felt through this than to say that we have been "held." Held in the hand of our loving Father.

If there was one thing that I could say got us through those difficult months, it would be this. We simply believed

God had a purpose for this. Did we *feel* like believing that? Absolutely not. But most of life is a decision. And we decided to believe.

Update on June 20, 2008

This is going to be a shorter update. Supper is waiting in the oven! Lowell is still in quite a bit of pain. We went to the ortho doctor down in Spokane on Tuesday. He is taking Lowell off of his old meds and trying some new. The new consist of an antiinflammatory, antidepressant, muscle relaxer, and a newer form of nerve med called Lyrica. We were advised about the antidepressant from a friend. Today is the third day he's been on that, and we are hopeful that it may be helping him. The pain hasn't been quite as constant today, coming more in surges again. So that is good! If I have my information correct, the antidepressant helps to heighten his pain sensitivity and also boost his mood, thereby enabling him to deal with the pain better. Lowell told me today that he thinks yesterday may have been the lowest point, so we are praying that it's all uphill from here on.

Nelson and Krista left today. We had eight little kiddos in the house here. It got rather noisy at times, but considering everything, it went very well. The cousins all had so much fun! We went through popsicles and milk like the kids thought there was going to be a shortage. Days consisted of running through the sprinkler, splashing in the wading pool, playing at the creek, eating popsicles in the grass, and having a picnic in the front yard. And, of course, there was the sandbox, swing set, and slide that got put to much use. Gotta go—the timer's beeping!

Update on June 24, 2008

The house is quiet for an hour right now while the little ones are all napping, so I am grabbing my chance to post another update about Lowell.

We are still waiting to get a call back from the pain clinic in Coeur d'Alene as to whether or not they will accept us and set up an appointment. If they decide to accept us, it will probably still be two weeks until we can get in. Lowell's ortho doctor referred him to this pain clinic to get an epidural steroidal injection. It's an injection (or series of injections) in the lower spine to help reduce his sciatic nerve pain. Sometimes it works, sometimes it doesn't. But it's worth a try right now.

On Sunday evening, his pain was pretty bad, and we called the ministers to see if they could come anoint him. They were glad to do it, and we felt at peace, knowing it is truly in the Lord's hands. He was not miraculously healed, but we believe God's will is being done in our lives. We believe Lowell, in his pain, will somehow be able to bring more glory to God than having been healed from it. We don't know how or why—we're just trusting Him.

Yesterday we went to see our family doctor here in Bonners Ferry. He was so very kind and talked with us quite a while about Lowell's meds and physical therapy. He put Lowell back on Dilaudid, which is something he was on in the hospital for pain. And he's also trying a different type of muscle relaxer. I don't know if his Lyrica is beginning to kick in or if the Dilaudid is helping that much, but today has been the best day we've had in a couple weeks. That's not to say he won't have some bad episodes yet. His nerve pain is different from all his other pain. It fades into the background for an hour or two, but then comes roaring back, leaving him almost shaking. I think he's done really well considering the amount of pain he's in.

As for the rest of us, we are having a really fine day. I was able to weed my garden and put down some mulch around the swing set. For me, that is called "playing"! We're learning to count the little blessings God gives us. It sure helps to keep our spirits up!

Update on July 8, 2008

Lowell is going to drive to town today! He has done it once by himself already, but he will be gone for several hours today. He wants to see if the chiropractor can help him at all. Then he also wants to stop at the worksite to get himself back in the swing of work again. He has been doing some office work/estimates here at home, although not like he normally does. His meds make it hard for him to think clearly and even see clearly. So we are also beginning to cut back a little on the meds to see if we can't help his vision and other side effects a bit. The pain is down to a bearable level. And for that, we praise our Lord! He has seen us through this far, and we are confident that He will continue to do so.

May you all have a blessed summer day!

Update on July 20, 2008

It is way past time for an update. We have been ex-tremely busy here the past couple weeks. Dennis Wurm came all the way from Indiana and surprised Lowell. I should say he "shocked" Lowell if you consider that Lowell's mouth fell open and he was rendered speechless. It was wonderful to have him here! Although, Jen, I'm afraid I spoiled him with fresh garden tea all week!

Then Kenny and Genny Graber came on Wednesday, along with Baby Benson. We have been having such a good time with them! We women have been just hanging out here at the house with all the babies and kiddos. We don't have much of a schedule, and our poor company actually gets cold cereal for breakfast most mornings. They assure me they don't mind, and I have no choice but to believe them. Genny made a mocha cheesecake for Sunday dinner today that is beyond scrumptious and was almost too pretty to eat.

Uncle Kenny and Aunt Rita came on Friday and will leave tomorrow morning. I think we've convinced them that two full days is not nearly enough time to take in all of North Idaho since Uncle Kenny just bought his Idaho elk tags for this fall.

Yesterday we took everyone up to the top of Black Mountain. That is one of the places where you can see for miles around, including Canada, Montana, and possibly Washington. That was a big milestone for Lowell! He has slowly been building up steam this week and did terrific yesterday. His stamina is improving daily, and he can be up longer than he has yet since the accident. His pain has been reduced tremendously from what it was 3–4 weeks ago. In fact, we have cancelled the pain-clinic appointment and will continue with his Lyrica for the time being.

We have so many things to thank God for! Lowell is feeling so much better, and we even got to go to Sunday School today. Just doing a few more of those "normal" things feels so good. He is even going to go flying this evening. Marcus Byler has agreed to take our company up in his plane so they can see Bonners Ferry from the air. Then we will make homemade ice cream for any and all who'd care to stop by!

We have an appointment with the ortho doctor on Wednesday, so I will try to get another update posted after that. Maybe, just maybe, he will say that Lowell is no longer an invalid!!

Throughout that summer, we had many visitors. Family and friends came thousands of miles to see us and help us carry our burden for a time. It was so wonderful to see them and helped give us a diversion from Lowell's pain.

It was with my uncle and cousin that we found the time to return to the scene of the accident up in Canada. It was a little more than three months after that day in May when we found ourselves standing at the edge of the ravine where God had decided to let our lives take a little detour.

Update on August 14, 2008

We finally went and visited the accident site last week when Uncle Greg and Caleb were here. I am so very glad they were along because without Caleb, we might not have been able to get Lowell out of that ravine. If you can call it a ravine ... it was really just a very steep drop-off to the lake. Pictures don't do it justice, but they do better than words.

It was almost traumatic, in a way, to go back there. All I'd ever heard was what the guys who were with him at the time told me. And I'd also seen the pictures they took. But to actually be there in person and slide down that very steep drop-off to stand where Lowell landed affected me deeply.

In all human reasoning, I should be a widow right now. There is no earthly possible way he could have flown that far off his bike down such a steep hill of boulders, missed so many trees and jagged rocks, and come out alive. After physically being there and seeing it with my own eyes, I can only say that God is good ... so very, very good.

Lowell went to the doctor yesterday and got a clean bill of health. It is now official—he can walk on his hip. Well ... let's say he can put weight on it. As for walking, that will take practice since his ankle still doesn't move well. Dan Coblentz

made him a cane to use, which has come in handy although I

don't dare tease Lowell about looking like an oldie-goldie.

He's liable to use his cane on me!

This will be the last update here on Carepages. I know

I've said that once before, but this is truly the last one. We feel

so very blessed to have been able to share with you all this sto-

ry of our journey this summer. Thank you for your prayers,

notes of encouragement, and also for you who gave to us fi-

nancially. God has met and will continue to meet our every

need.

*Give God room to work in **your** life ... and prepare to*

be amazed!

Looking back, we are not sorry that God allowed Low-

ell's accident. Even though Lowell still has some pain, and he

cannot walk without a limp yet, we do not wish it had never

happened. *To do so would be to turn our back on all the*

changes God has wrought in our hearts, souls, and lives. All those times I wanted to stomp my foot and yell, God had His finger of love in my heart and was gently wiping away my pride and selfishness. He knew what He was doing, and it was for my good.

"The Lord gave, and the Lord hath taken away; blessed be the name of the Lord." Job 1:21b

Chapter 18

My Altar of Tears

If there has been one dream I have held dear to my heart, it has been my dream of having lots of children.

I love babies. They are like precious little dew drops from Heaven. They smell sweet, look sweet, and feel sweet. Unless, of course, if you are the mom and must get up every two hours all night with them. Still, there is nothing more beautiful than a newborn baby, and my heart absolutely breaks for every woman who suffers with infertility. Their cross is a very silent, heavy one.

Even before I met Lowell, I had told my sisters I'd like to have a dozen children. After having four within five years, I changed my number to around eight. Now I was about to find out if God was thinking along the same line as I was.

Lowell had been on so many medications the past year that we had no idea how it had affected his body, especially when it came to fertility. In the early part of our marriage, we lost three precious babies, and that was a grief beyond words. I, in no way, wanted to visit that grief again. But, once again, it seemed as if God might have a different plan.

We decided we'd like to try for another blessing soon after the first of the year. I was so excited! In my human mind, it seemed as though I deserved a little happiness after the pain of the last year. I figured I had gone through just about all I could take. Surely now God would give me what I most desired.

Time passed and no baby was on the horizon. It was then that my deepest fear began to take root in my heart. What if this truly was permanent and God was saying He had blessed us enough? It was the idea of *permanently* that scared me out of my wits.

Would I be able to give it up?

Blinded by tears, I struggled with God while a fearsome battle raged within my soul. Why now when I wanted it so badly? Hadn't He asked enough of me out of the last year already? Why must He ask more?

This was *not* a part of my heart I wanted to give up. It was not as though I had asked for something selfish like a bigger house or nicer car. This was a baby, a child - a soul.

Grief overwhelmed me as I fought on. Weren't we entitled to a little happiness now? Just like Job, this was where we were supposed to be blessed. We had tried our utmost to glorify Him this past year, tried to smile through the tears, tried to carry His banner of love while we struggled to stand through our pain.

But this … this was too much.

God, my arms are weakening, my banner is going down. I cannot stand strong anymore.

It feels as if this valley will never end and the winter in my soul will last forever. I am so tired, so very tired. I have tried to give You the praise in everything thus far. I have believed that You were there even when You were silent. I be-

lieved that You had a reason for all this pain. So where is my blessing?

And then He brought me to the altar once again—my altar I had built of all my dreams and all my hopes. It seemed I had found myself at that altar so many times that it was wet with tears of grief that had been shed over and over again.

Then I heard His whisper. "You have praised Me in the midst of everything else this last year; why can you not praise Me in this?"

My head hung low.

Oh, God, not this dream. Anything else but this one, please. Only You know how much I want another child, how deeply embedded this dream is within my heart, and how truly agonizing it will be to give it up. It will be like ripping my heart out. Surely You cannot ask this of me. I feel as though You've asked so much that I have no more to give.

And still the altar awaited me and the gift of that one small part of my heart I had never been able to surrender. I saw more tears fall, but these were not my own. I looked across the altar at eyes so full of love.

Eyes that were shedding tears along with me. The hands reaching for my dream were nail-scarred and blood-stained. Deep within my soul, I wanted to please Him. I knew I could not go against Him.

He *was* my all, even when He *asked* for my all.

And in that moment, I prayed a prayer of desperation. One that we pray when we have absolutely no strength left of our own.

God, I want to lay it up on that altar. I want to say, "Not my will, but Thine be done." But I cannot. I want to say those words and mean them. I want to lift my arms up there, but they are so tired, so weak.

Tears coursed down my cheeks as I cried out. *Help me, God. For I cannot do it on my own.*

Then those nail-scarred hands reached down and lovingly lifted my weary arms to my altar of tears while, once again, His finger of love wiped away the pride and selfishness of my heart.

Sobbing, I whispered, *"I praise You even in this."*

Chapter 19

Broken Doesn't Mean Forgotten

"The sacrifices of God are a broken spirit: a broken and a contrite heart, O God, Thou wilt not despise." Psalm 51:17

I grew to love this verse when still in high school and have learned to appreciate it more with each passing year. And ever since my youth, I have wanted that verse to be me. I have wanted to be broken before my Lord so that He can use me in His own way.

I have seen many truly broken people within my short lifetime. And they are not a beautiful sight in the eyes of the world.

They are not the ones who seem to have it all together. They are not those whose lives seem perfect, their souls seem sinless, and those who seem to be natural heroes.

These broken people are a sorry lot to the world looking on. But they are the most exquisite, the most beautiful creatures in the eyes of our Father. *For they are the ones who have completely come to the end of themselves.*

King David is an Old Testament hero I have admired. When most people think of him, they think of a small boy facing a giant of staggering height. Or perhaps they remember his beloved psalms or how many enemies of God he annihilated or that he was in the lineage of the Messiah.

But do you know what I see when I look at David? I see a man so broken in pieces he cannot get up from the ground on which he has fallen. I see a man bathed in tears. Tears of regret and tears of shame. Tears of sorrow.

I see a heart completely and utterly broken before the Lord. And to think that this broken man was an adulterer, thief, and murderer.

Yet what does God say about him? He calls him "a man after mine own heart" (see Acts 13:22). He was a broken mass of humanity, yet the Lord calls him a man after His own heart.

After David's sin with Bathsheba and after the killing of Uriah was found out, he immediately fell to his knees in repentance. Psalm 51 is one of the most beautiful psalms ever written.

It was written by a repentant man before a holy God. It reveals the heart of a broken man. Verse three says, "For I acknowledge my transgressions: and my sin is ever before me." A broken person realizes that he or she is nothing without the blood of Jesus Christ.

These broken people today are the ones God has brought through fire and flood, and they have come out shining. They did not allow their circumstances to turn them into ever-growing lumps of bitterness. They did not allow their sin to keep them in the muck and mire, but they repented and were washed white as snow.

That is what I have desired all my life. To feel the Lord working in my heart, changing my heart, and drawing me closer to Him. *I have wanted to be broken.*

But God never told me it would hurt so much to be a broken person. He did not say that to completely and totally give up oneself would feel like a dagger in my heart. I knew it wouldn't be easy, but I didn't know it would hurt so much. Just like that piece of pottery, you must go through the painful fire of submission before you can become a beautiful vessel ready for use. And that fire hurts.

As you read in the last chapter, I was struggling with giving up a part of my heart that I had held onto selfishly for so many years. Like a child with a toy, I was afraid that, if I gave it away, it would never be given back. I struggled with God for several months, wanting to give it up, but I was afraid, so afraid.

Then it dawned on me what I had believed all through Lowell's accident. I had believed that God allowed that accident *for a reason.*

We do not serve a random God of chance and probability. We serve a God who does all things with a heavenly purpose in mind. Although we may not know the purpose down here on earth, there is still a reason known to Him.

And should this infertility prove to be permanent, it was for a reason known to my Lord. As I realized this, I was finally able to place it in His hands, bow my head, and say, "Not my will, but Thine be done."

Only when we have given up completely is God able to use us most efficiently. The Lord brought me to the place where I had to fall on my face before Him before He could lift me to my feet. And for that, I praise Him. It hurt like I have never hurt before.

But it didn't stop there. A broken person is not simply broken and left to lie in the dust. Yahweh Himself reaches down, brushes us off, and fills us with the sweetness of His presence that lingers through all eternity.

The giving up is well worth the peace that follows thereafter.

I had given Him my all, knowing that He had a reason. And I was at peace.

But God wasn't done.

A couple weeks later, I stood with tears once again streaming down my cheeks. For there in my hand was a strip with two pink lines.

The blessing had come.

The Final Chapter

Chapter 20

Just A Mom

Mom. Mother. Friend. Cook. Maid. Diaper changer. Bottle feeder. Bath giver. Ouchie kisser. Teacher. Story book reader. Barber. Kid dresser. Hair detangler. Dish washer. Manure hauler. Seamstress. Hug giver. Honorable judge in your own juvenile court. The list could go on and on. What is your job description? Do you consider yourself just a housewife or just a mom?

Satan has convinced this civilized world that a woman who is "just a mom" is nobody important. He says she must be out *doing* something important in order to *be* somebody important.

Look around you at every tangible thing you see that humans work so hard for every day, seven days a week. Look at the mounds of papers that executives go through on their way to the almighty dollar. Take a look at the mansions built for Hollywood actors in all their fame and glory. Or all the laws the government passes just to prove its far-reaching power.

Now I want you to take a look with me at my grandfather who was lying in a hospital bed almost two years ago. At the age of 43, he had had a stroke that left him paralyzed on the left side. Over the next four decades, he continued to decline until he was bedridden and longed to go Home to see his Lord.

Even though he was not able to talk and walk well, he touched more lives than he ever knew. His heart knew no bitterness, and his face was always alight with the joy that comes from knowing Jesus. He was not rich. He had no power or fame. But he touched other souls through the testimony of his life.

Look at him with me as he lay on his hospital bed struggling for his last breath. Did he have his arms full of money to take with him to eternity? Did he have important documents that said he was a person to be honored? Did he take trophies to prove his fame here on earth? No, we all know he didn't.

Instead, he was surrounded by souls who will follow him to Heaven when God calls their names. The Bible says in Job 1:21, "Naked came I out of my mother's womb, and naked shall I return thither."

Mothers, we are keepers of souls. You and your husband have *the* most important job in this world, and that job is to guide your children to the foot of the cross where they repent of their sins. Then we walk alongside them to eternity.

Do you not see how this is more important than any other career on earth? You take your children with you when you die. If you are leading a life down the path of sin, you are leading them straight to hell. But if you are leading them down the path of the blood of Jesus Christ, you are leading them to the cross and to Heaven.

I know how it is some days when you stand at your kitchen window with your hands in a sink full of dirty dishes, and it seems as though the world is passing you by. The times when you have swept the floor for the second or third time that day, and it feels as though that is all you do.

Mothers, those are the days the devil loves to whisper in your ear, "You are not important. You are *just a mom.*" He knows the exact moment when you will believe it most, and he will not pass up that opportunity to try and bring you down to his level. Down to where you begin to long for recognition in the eyes of the world.

From the moment your first child entered this world, God Himself gave you one of His most important positions, that of a mother.

A mother is one of His soul-gatherers. She spends twenty-four hours a day, seven days a week, with a special group of souls He has put in her charge. He has equipped her with all the necessary equipment to handle all the crises that will come her way. And He has given her a spirit so gentle that she can hear Him guiding her.

Never let the devil's lie take root in your heart—not for a moment. If you do, you will soon begin to look to the world for your fulfillment, and your marriage and children will become second place and, soon afterwards, second rate.

We not only take our children with us to eternity, but we also touch other lives through our children.

My husband is an avid hunter and especially loves to bow hunt. His sons are closely following in his footsteps if the box of bows and arrows in the basement are any indication.

When he takes out his bow at the beginning of the season, he takes extreme care with it, as well as with his arrows. He carefully sharpens each arrow tip and repairs any damage done during the previous hunting season. He cleans and fixes them until he is convinced that they have been groomed to the best of his ability. The fletching must be on just perfect so the arrows will fly straight. The tips must be razor sharp so they will pierce the target.

Then when it's time to hunt, he puts the arrows in his quiver, carries his bow on his arm, and heads out to look for the perfect target. Once he finds it, he puts his arrow in his bow, pulls back the string, and releases it. It sails through the air in a perfect line and pierces his target, exactly where he wanted it.

Our children are those arrows. We spend twenty years sharpening, repairing, smoothing, and cleaning them. When it's time to let them go, we aim them toward the target and let them fly. We may not even be able to see where they land, but we have done our job at aiming them toward eternity.

We also cannot see the lives they touch and the souls they gather with them along the way. Any souls they take to Heaven are souls you have touched as well, *because the touching came through the arrows you let fly.*

So the next time you are standing at your kitchen window and you hear Satan whisper that old lie in your ear, remember that those precious children you train today are the preachers, the churches, the teachers, the missionaries, the fathers, and the mothers of tomorrow.

"As arrows are in the hand of a mighty man; so are children of the youth" (Psalm 127:4)

About the Author

Kendra D. Graber lives in the rugged mountains of North Idaho where she strives to serve the Lord as a wife to her husband, Lowell, and the mother of five beautiful children. She enjoys writing and blogging, gardening and canning. Baking cookies is not just a chore, but a joy! Sledding in the winter is a highlight to their family, as are camping trips in the summer. In her spare time, she runs a small business from home. To learn more about this little family, you are welcome to visit their website at www.livingintheshoe.com.